Debbie:
Live your Passion...
Be your happiest...
Love!
Lori

Pivot Principal

A Principal's
Guide to Excellence

Lori Perez

ROWMAN & LITTLEFIELD EDUCATION

A division of
ROWMAN & LITTLEFIELD
Lanham • Boulder • New York • Toronto • Plymouth, UK

Published by Rowman & Littlefield Education
A division of Rowman & Littlefield
4501 Forbes Boulevard, Suite 200, Lanham, Maryland 20706
www.rowman.com

10 Thornbury Road, Plymouth PL6 7PP, United Kingdom

British Library Cataloguing in Publication Information Available

Library of Congress Cataloging-in-Publication Data

Perez, Lori, 1955–
  Pivot principal : a principal's guide to excellence / Lori Perez.
     pages cm.
  Includes index.
  ISBN 978-1-4758-0646-5 (cloth : alk. paper) — ISBN 978-1-4758-0647-2 (pbk. : alk. paper) — ISBN 978-1-4758-0648-9 (electronic) 1. School principals. 2. School management and organization. I. Title.
  LB2831.9.P47 2014
  371.2'012—dc23   2013040686

∞™ The paper used in this publication meets the minimum requirements of American National Standard for Information Sciences—Permanence of Paper for Printed Library Materials, ANSI/NISO Z39.48-1992.

Printed in the United States of America.

Contents

Preface

Today's principals feel overwhelmed by the journey that lies ahead of them. They sincerely want to transform their culture in order to shape consistently positive student, parent, teacher, staff experiences at their sites but the task feels daunting. With the right mind-set, their goals are achievable.

I am writing this book for the many good people who come into our position with great optimism but soon feel that they are merely paper shufflers and middlemen conveying the latest dictates from on high, tossed about in the sea of e-mails, phone calls, and social media. That, my friends, is *not* what being a leader is all about. Leaders successfully develop school cultures against tough odds. In short, the most critical of all leadership skills can be found in your own thinking. Developing and maintaining a compelling vision, having the guts and perseverance to withstand resistance, having a mind-set to be service centered and inspiring excellence through compassion and your own hard work is leadership.

To create a service-centered culture, start with a compelling vision, muster the courage within you, sharpen your analytical thinking skills, and fuel your passion for doing what's right.

This book is divided into eight chapters. The journey is in somewhat of a circle that takes you from reflecting on myths and truths about schools through taking action on planning, implementation, assessments, and developing your freedom to truly lead. The book pauses to acknowledge the challenges and joys within leadership, then picks up with cultivating your riches by providing a structure for success, one day at a time.

Throughout the book you will pause to take notes, reflect on your thinking, and plan for next steps. It is only through reflective practice and recognition of what works and doesn't work for you and your team that you will find ultimate success.

At the end you are guided to develop your own "Just Do It" plan. Without taking a first step, a marathon is never run. Now is your time to take hold of an opportunity to not just shape the lives of your immediate community but of the country and the world. Yes, you are *that* influential. Any less thinking is much too narrow in scope, limiting your ability to be effective in your position.

Acknowledgments

Without love, life, and laughter, a heart is devoid of songs. The simple fact is you have to follow your heart and believe. A leap of faith is powerful and takes deep courage. My freedom learned outside of the system can give power and strength to those still remaining within to take action for our future or be lost forever. Being the pivot is being bold enough to make a difference now.

Living in excellence with your learning community is understanding and working with the nuances of change every day; seeing it, breathing it, moving in the direction to benefit all children by being bold in your vision and passionate about inspiring those you influence. *You*, the principal, make the ultimate difference, not because of your knowledge of content or pedagogical theories, but by your ability to connect and collaborate with people. Connect and inspire for measurable, joyful results, be a pivot for excellence!

Thank you and with loving gratitude to:

Arthur A Perez

Taylor James Foster

And my mom, Verna Garey. . . . Because she has always believed in me, even
when I didn't believe in myself.

A Note to the Reader

I have three assumptions about you:

1. You are invested in the future of education
2. You want to personalize learning at every level of education
3. You are willing to work with the one person who can make the most positive gains in your school and your career, *you.*

If indeed my assumptions are correct about you, this book is for you; come on in. We will be exploring the immeasurable but palpable "soft skills" that will propel you to new heights of fulfillment and even joy including development your own good habits of thinking. You will learn how to work a plan for success. You will learn to recognize and develop the community riches of finance and staffing. You will be introduced to a structure for daily success to keep you balanced and flexible on the "sand" you will walk in everyday to practice excellence with team members across your community from students to leaders. Let's start with an analogy of water and education.

Think of a lake, a pond, even a fishbowl. All have the common elements of water, limits within and without its boundaries and life. The system of education is no different. The shiny surface is reflective of the life outside the body of water, not within itself. The ecosystem has no way of changing this pattern and function; to do so would mean the demise or collapse of the structure. A pebble dropped into the center or skipped from the edge ripples through the entire system, causing greatest change in the immediate area of impact and continuing throughout until the last of the water's edge has felt its movement. The water itself cannot cause change above or below its surface without the introduction of an outside force before settling back to the glossy surface reflecting the potential of the outside world. A lake, a pond, even a fishbowl, mirrors the life outside its defined confines, so like the educational system within which I have worked for nearly thirty-five years.

The reforms of recent years have demanded that "the system" look within itself to reflect upon rituals and routines that complete the balance of nature within education. The reforms have not given the life within the boundaries of this delicate ecosystem the tools to accomplish the task satisfactorily, for there are few real rituals and routines that truly are worth repeating. My favorite quote I heard so often in the district hallways is "if the horse is dead, get off and walk." The truth is education as we know it simply can't get off its horse, it's been dead a long time.

Built on the now failed top-down business models of old, education is simply stuck. The traditional public education model does not have a model outside the structure that has protected the weak, pushed out the bold, and forced the innovative to continually reinvent the same message. Eventually even the most optimistic will feel their spirit fade into resignation, submission or early retirement.

With all the purpose of the pebble skimming itself across the surface before plunging into the heart of the pond, landing on the bottom only to raise the surface a fraction of a fraction, I write this book. To bring the courage to share what works to those who will listen. The ripples are inching ever closer to spilling onto the land at the water's edge, pebbles are gathering at the bottom.

Understanding that trees grow in dirt, water must be absorbed into the land; what is left will be evaporated into the air. This evaporated water will regroup again as gathering rain clouds, dropping into the next pond, and it will wait until enough pebbles fall into this pond to raise the water up to the surface and begin the cycle again. From a stagnant pond grows beautiful life and new clouds of promise. The land can truly feed and nourish the roots of young saplings as they absorb water, not the other way around. A sapling will die plunged directly into the water; the water must be routed to that sapling. So too, then, education must be moved to the students and their families. This is the fallacy of old thinking in the culture of today.

Following the water cycle model idea, education must meet the learner in his or her own learning environment. The lakes (schools) and ponds (classrooms) within the ocean of education must find the fissures below or the edges above to leach the salt and cleanse its essence before entering into the roots of the young plants eagerly waiting their nourishment and life-sustaining quality. We cannot sit calmly within the water of our comfortable lake reflecting on the potential of the world and believe for a minute that we are making a difference on the environment. We are not.

Children are growing into adults with shallow root systems, willowy branches, and immature leaves. They have not developed the life skills to confidently move into an undefined future because the adults in their lives are not living boldly in their truth to move the water!

In conclusion, within the current system people truly have been discouraged from working together, from introducing a pebble, so the lake remains intact to feed its own ecosystem, all the while starving the life around it. The joy and optimism of creativity have been lost. That is no way to live your life. It certainly isn't a way I could ultimately thrive.

My son and husband are both unique, just as I am, with needs that the typical system would have failed if not for the gentle hands of those that bucked the system to lift us out of the murky water of our stale lakes to do something extraordinary, each to be a pebble upon the glossy surface that changed our lives forever by sharing their joy and passion.

Be that gentle hand for those who follow. Throw your own pebbles; create the ripples that will ignite continuous learning for our children and those who practice our craft. Walk in excellence with your community; uncover its passions, challenges, and fears; celebrate life and learning with them.

Whether a child or adult, in a "school community" we are all searching for excellence, learning from each other. After all, "community" *is* a group of people living together in one place practicing common ownership. In other words, you are continually reestablishing excellence with your team; why not make that time joyful and powerful?

It is important that you never lose your ability to see the big picture, to keep your compass headed true north, even when the road ahead may be closed. You possess the ability to change humankind, one person at a time. And truly, that is what it takes, looking at and defining what each person needs in your own ecosystem to be joyful and competent. I believe our collective job is that big, to change the world. No effort is worth your time and energy unless you see the opportunity within that effort being bigger and better than what you have now.

At the conclusion of each chapter use the mapping exercise to think about the content and what you want to do with the information. Understanding your pivotal role and connector being the conduit between the outside and inside of your community is key to moving your team together as one system of excellence.

The information may resonate with you, prompting immediate action. Or the content may be something you connect to other ideas you are exploring. Alternatively, the content maybe something that will bring you back at a later time to ponder and develop into action.

The only way to improve our system is to take personal responsibility for the children, parents, teachers and *you*. Be bold in your joy and sincere in your passion. People will believe in your vision and work if you first believe in yourself.

Chapter One

Eight Myths in Schools
and Three Truths about You

This chapter will lead you to think about the system as a whole, not just your school. It is important to realize that the general population thinks about school probably more than you realize and perpetuates their opinions through their own myths about education. Because of this thinking and the fact that most people have experienced school as their own reality based on their attendance once upon a time, myths have real feelings attached to them. It may sound kind of silly, but these myths drive political decisions at every level of society. At the end of this chapter you will have time to reflect on your own thinking and the myths you may be harboring subconsciously, to consider what you will do with that thinking, and how to put it into action.

1. SCHOOLING IS CHILD'S PLAY

Truth is, often the adults are "at play."

Adults are practicing everyday on children in the schools; therefore, they are "at play." More often than not administrator types spend a lot of money purchasing a program that is "research based" only to discover that the program doesn't work with "their" kids. Why? It is not because the children are different, it is because the structure of the program is different. After working with several adoptions in different school districts, I understand how this works.

Teachers select materials based on their own strengths and programs, which vary from teacher-to-teacher within the same grade, within the same school. These programs grow out of the experiences the teachers have had;

what a neighbor has done in the past; and most of all, what feels comfortable to the teachers. Truth is, students actually have very little to do with it.

Teachers and administrators don't want to take the time to learn how to use the materials as they were intended, or worse, to even look at the data of their own community to determine what is truly needed. In fact, the more the materials appear to be familiar to the teacher, the more the teacher will like it, because then, under the guise of "professional judgment," teachers feel empowered to pick-and-choose the parts of the program they want to implement.

So, many times teachers will ask for training on materials and then, when all is set up, they won't attend the training. Why? The training would then mean that personal practices would have to change.

Principals don't take the time to get to know the materials or their students either. Why? Somehow, they feel it is not their job. A CEO of a large company would not fully understand how and why his or her staff does their job. As a principal, teacher, and parent, it is necessary to understand what the outcomes of the program are intended to be. It is necessary to know how much time should be devoted to the program and it is necessary to provide adequate resources for teachers to implement the program. Don't leave it up to the teachers to tell you what the program is or isn't and don't expect them to ask for help.

As the leader, you need to structure opportunities for teachers to share with you one-to-one what is working in their opinion. It is also necessary for you to regularly observe what is being taught. Expect what you inspect—nothing less. Look at student work and results. Is it what you expect? Why not? Start to unpeel the onion of curriculum.

There is plenty of latitude for teachers to add their own personal touch to an approved instructional program. Teachers must work together as grade-level teams in planning, assessing, and sharing if we ever hope to break the cycle of "playing" with the curriculum and the resources to instruct. Never allow people to be islands unto themselves.

The instructional program is not for the teachers; it is for the children. As adults, we must always consider what is best for the students; often, that is not the most convenient or easiest option for the adults. Remember that the routines should remain the same throughout the system; the personal rituals can be flexible. For example, the routine of a reading lesson should be the same, the ritual of where to sit may be different.

2. EVERYONE KNOWS WHAT AN "A" MEANS

Truth is, we all have our own meaning.

The great debate about grades will never end. Adults who have gone to school within the American system of education are comfortable with the classical A–F system that has been used for years, particularly if they were at the top end of the alphabet. The problem with that is people don't agree on what an "A" is and especially don't agree with what a "C" or an "F" means.

Somehow we have twisted a fairly straightforward system that held the notions of "superior," "average," and "failing," with variations on the theme, into one that has two levels of appropriate "A" or "B" and everything else as substandard. When you consider your own child or family member, admittedly you have to agree that if they get a "C" you consider them (or the teacher) as doing something substandard. So, how should we evaluate student performance?

The only real way to get away from grading nonsense is to understand exactly what we want students to learn. We need to identify acceptable performance goals. These need to be communicated to students, parents, and staff; all must maintain the same expectation to move the system forward. This is where samples of rubrics and effective practice sharing have become so powerful.

Take the example of the child learning how to play the piano. The teacher often plays a piece for the student so the child can hear what the piece sounds like, can feel the music and appreciate the quality and tone. Without providing models, children often grope in the dark trying to determine what is expected. If teachers and parents don't share with children the expectation and simply say "try harder" or "do your best," you are counting on the fact that the child has some innate ability to second-guess you; often this is not the case, especially for children learning the structure of English in addition to performing grade-level tasks.

As the leader, keep models from one year to the next, share models from class to class, review personal portfolios with children so they can see their own progress over time. Compare a child's work with an acceptable model, don't make anyone guess at what is suppose to be practiced and mastered.

An easy way to engage learners directly is to provide practitioners with a model. I love to read with young students who are struggling. Rarely, if ever, have these children even heard what the reading should sound like. So I simply say, "make your voice sound like mine." You would be amazed. This holds true for writing as well, "make your writing sound like this." Children will be anxious to share their success with you, and teachers will appreciate your working alongside them, not above them or despite them.

Make sure there is time weekly for teachers and administrators to look at student work together, to identify what "grade-level" appropriate practice is and share this with parents regularly. The most powerful parent conferences are held with samples of student work, both a child's and their classmates. It speaks volumes to a parent when they compare their own child's work with that of a class peer. Immediately parents know if the child is advanced, behind, or "just right," at grade-level, without much guidance on the part of the teacher or principal. Your time can then be spent developing a plan that includes the school and home in advancing the child to the next level of practice. From my point of view it seems to make sense that children perform at different levels of practice, just like adults in real jobs do.

Children are all novices promoted to varying levels of proficiency until they can demonstrate mastery over the grade-level content, which comes at the end of year for most. For those who master the content earlier, a program to advance them should be determined along with the parents, not additional busy work assigned. Spend time looking at the real skills children need, life skills. Evaluating reading writing, and math are important, but just as important are presenting an idea, supporting a position, and working cooperatively in a group. Content just isn't something that can be "assigned" any longer in our society of instant information. How to evaluate content, find resources, and develop presentations in novel ways seem to be the new content worthy of our learners time.

These approaches work for teachers too. Just think about it. Use the parent conference strategy in developing a plan to take the teacher to the next level of his or her practice. Rarely, though, does a teacher move from novice to a level of proficiency in just one year. It takes years of committed effort to perfect the level of practice that we all desire, and only through carefully placed questions and follow-up on your part will your teachers be propelled to greatness. Your goal here is to coach every teacher to greatness.

The public does not want good teachers for their children, they desire *great* ones. That's an "A" in anyone's book!

3. DON'T SMILE UNTIL CHRISTMAS

Truth is, if learners don't connect to their teachers right away, they probably won't, and the desired learning will not be achieved. If learners (children and adults) don't connect with you as the leader of the community, you will never create the team you desire.

This is where passion resonates. Education is not just about content standards and levels of practice, but is an artful interplay of communication and connections. Teachers need to connect with their students, and principals need to connect with their teachers, simple as that. Without these human connections trust will not be established. To say that we have undervalued this human link in education is an understatement. We have professed the positive aspects of diversity, but we have not taken the time to develop the common core values needed in order for people to trust each other.

If the "soft skills" of developing personal relationships, character, and attitude do not come naturally to you, work on them. They are the keys to a well-run, thriving learning community. Your "hard skills" (education, interview techniques, and writing) may get you the position but it's your sharing of those vulnerable "soft skills" that will allow you to lead your team successfully.

Schools typically have not reached out to the communities in which they reside to know the lay of the land. How many principals or teachers visit homes these days? How many times have you conducted a community forum just to find out about the community? How many times have you introduced yourself to the local community leaders and sought their input on the school that is on their block of business or next door to their house? How many times have you just sat down for a cup of coffee and talked to a parent? Invite someone to coffee or whatever social venue suits you and just talk about education.

The people you interact with may or may not be associated with your school, but everyone has an opinion about schools and education. Your goal is to ask simple questions.

- What should the ideal school look like?
- What traits did your favorite teacher possess?
- What did you hope to learn in schools that you didn't?
- If you could talk to my teachers/students, what would you share?
- What should be *my* mission today to make a difference for kids tomorrow?
- How will you know education is improving?

The public "gets it," but educators do not when it comes to community. The local Chamber of Commerce and Board of Realtors certainly understand the subtle nuances of "networking," yet educators seem to bury their heads in the sand, professing they just have too much work to do within the school to ever leave the campus. Here are four activities worthy of your time.

- Attend a networking social in your community.
- Ask people (especially parents) what their opinions are about what works and doesn't work locally.
- Show the community that you are invested in their future through affiliation with a local service organization.
- Share your story.

Service organizations would love to have school people involved in their clubs, for it gives them a link to children and the future. Oftentimes service clubs go looking for projects to fund and support with time and effort simply because they don't know the educational system, no one has invited them "in" with a good story and a simple smile. Don't be defensive about what you do, be joyful in your tales of individual success and team-building activities.

Education has failed to develop a sense of community within the community it serves. In essence, there is little trust between a community and a school that merely exists within it if you don't make an effort to become a part of "we." Why? As the leader you need to share the "soft skills" of relation building, demonstrating character, and joyfully expressing an attitude of success. If you are excited about what you are doing, others will be too. Get excited and share. It's fun and profitable.

Do the unexpected; be "real" to your families. Go to a performance or pancake breakfast you are invited to, comment on a Facebook entry, watch a video and send a quick note; as a matter of fact, write *lots* of "thank you" notes. Whether formal or informal, handwritten notes are appreciated and noticed. Connect, connect, connect; and smile, smile, smile.

4. TO FAIL IS TO LOSE SELF-ESTEEM, DETERMINATION, AND DRIVE

Do not believe this for one minute. As a first-grade student, I remember my mother attending a conference with the teacher. The teacher said I was a nice girl but wasn't college material. I remember hearing that conversation when I was six, more than fifty years ago. Being a child who wanted to please my mom and others, I felt compelled throughout my schooling to prove that teacher wrong. I took the challenge of a potential failure and made it a crusade. Many children do this instinctively if we are frank with them.

- What is wrong with showing children what needs to be improved and accomplished?
- What is wrong with ensuring understanding at one level before moving on to the next?

Every child is different and nothing ever holds true in every situation but take a look at what is going on in society.

The upwardly mobile parents understand the importance of every educational advantage. It is a common practice to "hold a child out" of school until they turn six in many communities so that the child can have an additional year of preschool or can begin to learn the fundamentals of reading independently from "the system" so that the child can have an advantage heading into the competition of the school structure.

Even more pronounced is the number of teachers who hold their own children back in grade school until they have mastered the skills necessary to be successful in the following grades. Why do we keep these options from others? We are a public system that must adapt to the individual. Individuals walk and talk at different times, they will always read and write at different times as well.

Failing is a natural part of learning. Nothing can be accomplished unless we try; failure often leads to increased understanding, a new concept, a better way. As educators we are by nature "nurturers." Nurturing has everything to do with failure. If a child fails at something, isn't it appropriate to show him what to do, comfort him, become a guide for him? Ask questions, look for connections, try again. Deep down you want someone to nurture your learning, talent, dreams and aspirations. Why must education insist on false accolades, best tries and non-competitive activities when the society we send children into is filled with the opposite? That disconnect with real life is just coming to light.

Don't you think "trust" has a little something to do with this conversation? Students and parents will trust you if you tell them the truth, even if it may sound negative or harsh to you. Pleading with my son's teachers to let me know when he did something inappropriate or missed an assignment instead of letting him slip by until the inappropriate behavior became a pattern. Time and again, into high school, I would have to wait to "discover" a shortcoming through a report card, not a phone call, e-mail or personal note. How much trust did I have for those teachers and principals? They didn't follow through simply because they didn't want to be the bearer of bad news, or in my mind, it was because they didn't really care. It is our job to be honest with children and parents. They will trust and support us if we trust and support them.

The desire to excel is deep within us all. It is human nature to compete, with each other and with ourselves. Trying to improve over present performance is the highest form of competition, the real competition that needs to be nurtured within every child and team member.

5. PRACTICING FOR A TEST IS CHEATING

Truth is, in real life seldom is the outcome unknown when you are learning something new or improving your skills.

I remember my piano lessons. I was supposed to practice half an hour each day, and when I did, I improved. How is anything else different?

Many people profess that practicing for a test is cheating. It is only cheating in school. It is a best practice outside of the school walls. Of course you review questions for your driver's test prior to taking the test. You know that the format will be multiple choice, you study the guide book so you know all the laws, and you particularly pay attention to the newest laws because you know that "they" are going to try to trick you on those. Now this kind of studying doesn't mean that you are going to dismiss everything you know about good driving when you get behind the wheel and that you won't automatically adjust to a situation as needed down the street. School tests are no different. Why must we keep tests a secret from the children expected to take them and their parents?

Parents with the know-how will search the Internet to find clues for their children when it comes to taking just about any test. They will hire tutors and buy practice books. Often times they will construct problems at home with the same format as the upcoming test. Why do we keep these strategies away from other children? Look at the SAT test. There are several website tutorials for students set up by the company that writes the test. There are flash cards available for language, grammar, and math. There are classes, one or two days, even six weeks long, to help students prepare for the test. The SAT is the test that students must take for college entrance. Notice that students can choose the method to study—intense short-term or extended small steps.

Why do we have a different practice in grade school? Why don't we offer multiple ways for students to study and prepare for a variety of tests? Why must all students do things the same way? They shouldn't have to, really; it isn't logical. We need to be flexible in the way we offer tests and preparation. We need to take ownership for the "test anxiety" many children and parents feel because we don't offer them a way to prepare and feel confident. Confidence breeds success, and you know how that spirals. Confidence comes from the feeling of competence.

Develop competence in your students, families, and team members.

- Provide models
- Provide templates

- Provide steps or instructions
- Provide ways to measure growth
- Provide support
- Provide a smile and an ear
- Celebrate their efforts when milestones are observed

6. EDUCATORS KNOW WHAT'S BEST FOR CHILDREN

Truth is, if we actually knew what was best, wouldn't the results be better?

No one knows exactly what works best in all situations. You can make a good stab at a prediction based on the past, but until it is tried with a particular child we are never quite sure. Teachers and administrators base many of their conversations with children and parents on the fact that they won't challenge the authority you wield. The honest truth is that we really don't know and often base our advice more on ritual and past practice than fact.

Educators need to be "savvy" to the ways of the world. Understand that there is no harm in admitting that we might not have the answer right now. It is OK to seek advice from others and to learn from them. After all, we are supposed to be creating lifelong learners in our classrooms; we should be models of that practice.

One of the best ways to "offer advice" is to ask questions. Not only does it engage the other person in a two-way conversation but it gives you a glimpse of what they are expecting and exploring.

Do this; take some time by asking questions.

- Ask what the intended outcome is.
- Ask what they have done to attain the outcome.
- Ask how they are feeling about the goal.
- Ask what they want from you.

As educators with a "fix-it" mentality rarely do we take the time to find out what people really want from us. Sometimes it is just to listen and validate, not to offer yet another detour on their ultimate path of self-awareness and accomplishment. People are joyful when they feel they are in control and competent.

In your role as leader of your learning community and to create your ultimate joy and fulfillment, be the conduit to other people's successes.

7. IF PARENTS JUST CARED MORE

Truth is, parents do care; parents just don't know the system and the crazy doublespeak of educators.

Parents care about their children; they love them. They want what is best for their children, but frankly, they don't trust us as much as each other, their families, or neighbors. Why is this? It is because we give them "doublespeak." Often we are not open and honest with them because we fear their reaction.

Parents need help to understand their multiple roles in each child's life. It is their job to encourage vibrant, creative life in their children. We need to support the efforts of these well-intending parents to encourage their children to make something of themselves and to contribute something worthwhile to society. Parents have the ability for enthusiastic persuasion that no one else possesses. Parents can build fires in children's minds, fires that get them moving or fires that will burn out. We need to provide positive kindling for their fires.

Through parent education programs geared at helping to set home routines; asking appropriate questions; playing learning games; and properly motivating their children with time, experiences, and support we give the parents the keys to success for their children. Be enthusiastic about life! It is the key we all need to open the door of possibility.

Parents need the encouragement to not be vending machines for their kids. We all have a tendency to give things rather than to share our time. Throwing money (providing things) at children is only a temporary fix, whether at home or in school. Spending time setting up progressive chores and challenges, being there when things aren't perfect—these are what develop resiliency, empathy, and character.

As schools, institutions of learning, we need to see our role as directors of an orchestra with instruments just waiting to be played in harmony. Left alone with no director, the melody is lost to screeches of individual pieces of brass and wood that have nothing in common. Create your concerto by starting with parents. Listen to them, feel them, fill them with what they need so they can support education at home.

There are effective ways to care for parents so that they can care for their children successfully.

- Provide tools for parents. Assist them in seeing their many roles as a parent, not just a provider and coach but a cheerleader, a doctor, a teacher, a guide, a mentor, a chef, and a spiritual advisor.
- Remind parents that "parent" is an active verb, not a noun. To parent is to love, support, challenge, and develop a child.
- Connect parents with like-minded parents. Don't be afraid to connect parents so they may learn from one another. There is nothing worse for a parent than to feel like they are failing and there is no one to talk to for support. And, because of adult egos, more times than not this painful feeling is left unsupported, unrecognized, and unsolved, which does not ultimately help children succeed.
- Share resources on topics of their interest, not yours. Ask parents about what they want to know. Follow parent blogs, Facebook groups, and forums. It's all right there if you take the time to find out what the "hot topics" are for your community of parent learners.
- Develop trust in them before you can expect them to trust you. Take the time to meet parents. Offer well-placed personal stories of your own experiences or those of others you know. Offer to find information and share with them. Trust a parent before they trust you and you will have an ally in the education of their children.
- Develop trust in *yourself* before anyone else. Understand that you are the leader of the pack. Be that leader and step out with bold confidence, not arrogant righteousness. Doing the right thing for kids often means checking your ego at the door and believing in your ability to make a difference; now that is joy.

8. TEACHERS WANT TO BE
LEFT ALONE IN THEIR CLASSROOMS

Teachers, like every community, want a leader, someone who will make a decision, celebrate them for their gifts, and encourage them to be more.

People will follow your vision and lead if you have your facts straight and are decisive and caring. The worst thing a leader can do is stay in his office all day and avoid real decision making and conversations, opting for shuffling paper and filling out reports.

Use your senses for good. Listen to what is being said in your hallways; look into the eyes of everyone you are in contact with; smell and feel the air in a room; and taste life with those around you. More times than not the scent of uneasiness, the taste of disapproval, and the feel of dis-ease are palpable sensations that outsiders experience just by walking into a room or onto a campus or by observing a conversation. These may sound intangible to you, but that's the point, you have to rely on your intuition and general common sense to be purposefully joyful in the halls of your school.

Use all of your senses, not just your vision and hearing when leading your team. The most successful leaders feel what their teams feel and let them know that they know. Empathy, excitement, personal stories, and vulnerability as a person make you real to your community. The true leader will then follow up, using that information gained through all senses.

Knowing the right time is an acquired skill that comes with practice. It may be an immediate question, a follow-up conversation, sharing a frank observation, or a quick note. Whatever you do, don't ignore your intuition. It is your best friend and accomplice in leading joyfully.

Be clear about the options you have together. To be your most persuasive self with your team you need to be in the moment with them. Without that immediate presence you will end up with team members who have checked out and are half engaged. In other words, you will have lost your ability to influence your team. Be aware of what they need to keep moving forward, and then fill their buckets.

So now you have it, the myths about school and education that I have considered for the longest time. What can you do about them personally and which myths do you recognize out there? Read on and *say this out loud*:

I am capable of leading change,
I can make a difference,
I will focus on children,
I believe there is a better way!

ESTABLISHING YOUR PIVOTAL TRUTHS

Three simple actions that all principals must take to be successful.

1. Be kind
2. Work hard
3. Dream BIG

Be kind in all your dealings, at school, at home, in your professional and personal lives. Living the kindness you want your staff and students to develop is the first step to your success. Be kind and people will return the favor. Believe it, live it—so much easier said than done. At times doing for children despite the poor behavior of their parents or teachers is tough; in your mind the "bad behavior" won. In the long run though, showing kindness and grace demonstrates the true vulnerability of a confident leader.

Be bold in your kindness. Some people will look at you shaking their head in disbelief, but you will be confident that you did the right thing for a child. That unshakable boldness in demonstrating grace and kindness makes a leader great, makes *you* great and brings you joy. No one will ever fault you for doing a kindness, providing a smile and a nod of the head, lending a willing ear or a bend in a rule; these "kindnesses" don't cost a thing, but they are invaluable in your dealings with people. And, should you come up with someone who doesn't "approve," just know that there are some people in this world who are not happy with who or what they are. Grant them grace, fill them with your kindness, and move on.

There are so many more people in the world who will follow you and like you because you are kind, friendly, and fair. Ultimately, kindness is caring. Care about who you work with and for on a daily basis.

Working hard and keeping your balance are your guideposts. When asking new principals what was the one thing they didn't know before accepting the job, they said "the hours," "the paperwork," and "the people work."

It's hard work to be "on" all the time, but that is what you must do. Be prepared to fake it on your less-than-stellar days, smile at yourself in the mirror every day, and say out loud in your strongest voice, "Today is a great day." You are the compass of your campus—keep the "true north"; be vigilant in your quest to work smart, which can be hard work albeit rewarding beyond expression. Keeping people inspired, encouraged, and motivated is an endless job; you need to be many things to different people. Make connections for others, listen actively, and celebrate with your team.

To successfully navigate the "people work" that truly drives the hours and the paperwork as well, you must first deal with yourself. You are the most important person in your sphere of influence. If you haven't convinced yourself by now that you are worth investing time in and that you can make a difference, trust me, you won't be leading anyone else to feel that way either.

Do these things for yourself.

- Connect more with life. Not e-mails, phones, computers and "stuff." Life means living. Connect with living things that inspire you, make you laugh, bring you joy.
- Feel better. Take care of yourself. Get rest, eat the right foods, and move your body to equip yourself with all your senses.
- Ignite your passion. Do what brings you joy.

Dream BIG. If you see something that needs to be done, set the wheels in motion. Who better than you, the leader of your campus, to start a new project, to inspire others, to create momentum? You are the motherboard in this intricate circuitry of a community. See your school community as a "whole community."

You are the heart at the center of this living organism called school. You pump the ideas through the cardiovascular system of the body. Without you, the heart, nothing is pumped, primed, and working. Be bold, write down your big dream, whether for increased student enrollment, staff engagement, funding, or test scores. Remember that the ideas of every inventor started with a dream.

What will be your big, bold mission today? While many people in coaching will encourage to you take small steps forward, why not have the belief that you can take a giant leap for mankind? "Big leaps inspire, small steps tire."

Get a drink of water, take a walk, then sit down to think about the ideas presented. Jot down your ideas in the boxes provided. By the time you are done, you will have an action plan. This template may be copied and used multiple times for more than one thought.

Chapter 1   Reflections on Myths and Truths
Time_____ Date_____

What am I thinking about?	Why am I thinking about it?
What do I want to accomplish?	How can I get there?
Tools/support/people I need:	How will I recognize success?
How will I celebrate?	When will I think about this again?

What do I need to do to ensure my success; whom do I need to connect with?
How will my mentor(s) know I need support/help?

Chapter Two

Plan

There's an old saying that goes something like "plan the work and work the plan; fail to plan and you will fail." Nothing is truer in education. A game plan, an outcome, an objective, a goal, all have one thing in common, there is something tangible at the end.

Teaching is not just opening a book or clicking a button then sharing content with students. The human element—of understanding, working toward a goal, working through a challenge, devising a product together—is powerful.

- Do your students know what is expected of them? Do they know when they have accomplished the objective?
- Do they have ownership in their showing what they know?
- Have you set up your teachers to have these ideas in mind at the start of every lesson?
- Do parents ask the right questions of their children?

WHO BETTER TO LEAD THIS SHIFT THAN YOU?

This chapter will assist you in developing and working "your plan." For all the many written papers, articles, and books about "the plan" to follow, a plan is just a thing; it is not a living community. You first need to consider the resources you have at your fingertips and how to best utilize them. They may or may not fit into a published plan.

Know your "mine," the place where you work and learn every day. Polish your gems, recognize the many facets of your team members, and start building for success. Often schools fail because they try to be something they are not. Even though schools will pay thousands of dollars to get a system of best practices instituted, many more will fail than succeed because the community they are working with is not the community that was represented in the model.

Just as every fingerprint is unique, each learning community is unique. As a part of your ultimate plan you need to know your team from teachers and supporters, to students and parents.

NO ONE IS AN ISLAND

Often the act of teaching is conducted behind the walls of a classroom that few others really have access to. Most teachers work independently, in a "private practice," so to speak, rather than a collaborative learning environment. Let's make a comparison here. In a teaching hospital doctors take fellow student-doctors on rounds to observe, look at the data, and make a diagnosis. They confer together to write the prescription.

Do we do anything remotely similar to "grand rounds" in education? Probably not, which is a shame, because we learn the most from other practitioners, not from doing the same thing over and over again by ourselves. The notion of "grand rounds" was shared with me by a brilliant educator and mentor many years ago. Practice "grand rounds" with your staff. There are a couple of ways to do this successfully, building confidence and trust throughout your team.

Building grand-rounds conversations into staff meetings is an approach worthy of note. A staff member brings a student scenario for discussion. No names need to be used, no identifying features, so to speak. But what is important to share is the data about the child. Factual data from all types of assessments can be shared in a few short minutes. Then the concern for the learning can be shared openly followed by any steps the teacher has taken to this point. Staff members have time to ask questions and give suggestions. The teacher sharing the student listens, asks for clarification and now has new suggestions to ponder in prescribing the best course of learning for the child.

Remember the diagnostic/prescriptive teaching of the 1970s and 1980s? The difference here is that staff members are sharing real strategies with each other, not just looking at data on a piece of paper. This is a powerful way to introduce new techniques to teachers. A teacher can then report back at the next meeting any of the strategies that were tried and the progress the student is making. This "grand-rounds" practice is a perfect way to start staff meetings and a wonderful way to introduce staff members to fresh ideas.

Another take on grand rounds that is powerful is to take a teacher or two with you when you walk through the halls daily. Talk about what you are seeing, what the teachers are doing, what the students are doing, how the classroom feels. It is important for people to know how and where you are making connections to the pedagogical and content pieces of learning. Not only do the teachers walking the rounds with you learn and trust, but so do the teachers that you are recognizing by highlighting their practices.

We all want to feel competent. When your principal acknowledges your work in a particular area of teaching, wow, that's a powerful trust-building, joyful technique.

IT'S ALL FOR ONE AND ONE FOR ALL

A teaching learning community is no different from any sport team in terms of shared goals, and this idea is worthy of consideration. People like to be a part of something with energy. When an organism, a team or group, moves forward together the entire system feels the movement top to bottom, side to side, head to toe; yet, if one person moves forward from a group, it is barely felt or noticed by the whole. Or worse yet, the one person will be isolated and rejected by the whole. Why? Because the team is not moving forward together. Movement together is the power.

Think of this in your picture for staff development for a minute. Effective staff development is not singularly sending someone off to a conference or having an expert come in for a day. But rather, what is done with the information after it has been introduced; now that's the power of the learning.

When you send someone off to get trained in a methodology or learn a new strategy, ask yourself these questions:

- How do I ensure that the information is shared with everyone?
- Does this person now become the "guru" of the strategy? How can I develop that notion in them before the group?
- Do I allow time for others to see the teacher in action?
- Do I allow meaningful time for the person to "coach" others on the staff?
- Do I encourage this person to move out of their comfort level to move beyond the group in this area?
- How do I make this happen?

We need to not only become aware of the shrinking resources we have but to understand they aren't coming back. Staff development needs to be just that—*staff* development, not individual development. Developing a single person and leaving the overall team the same is not a practice that has fared well. It leads to resentment, isolation, and ultimately burnout.

Take the time to develop your school plan and then work it. When your plan includes staff development, make sure that the information gets out to everyone. A handout from a workshop won't work, neither will an announcement in a bulletin or a quick mention at a staff meeting; there is no personal connection to those inanimate objects.

Build the strategy you select with your team members, then follow-up in your own personal calendar. Build your calendar to include follow-up practice and demonstrations. Include time for people to discuss the strategy and ask questions. As the instructional leader, you need to be able to have the big picture of your school. You need to have a handle on what comes into that environment and how it is used. Consider the role of a chief executive officer for a moment.

A CEO of a large company does not allow individuals to bring new ways of doing their job into the organization without careful consideration of the impact on the whole. Remember, you are the one in charge, leading the team, directing the orchestra. You should have the ability and with-it-ness to know what practices are used for which purposes on your campus. The public expects that of you.

Don't be afraid to ask leading questions of your team. "I noticed you are using _____ for your reading instruction with these children. Talk to me about your selection." While your job is not to micromanage your team, your job is to see that the team is working together toward the common vision of excellence you have established.

NO TIME TO BE A LONER

At this point, no one has the time to be a loner. Effective communication skill development is the key: this goes for your team members as well as you, the principal. Two things need to take place to ensure that everyone is communicating effectively. First, you need to communicate openly and honestly with integrity. Second, you need to listen effectively, openly, and with integrity.

Generally, if you asked them, people in leadership roles don't have tremendous difficulty communicating. Where the problem lies is in the vulnerability of doing it "openly, honestly, and with integrity." When decisions are required, often one right after the other, it becomes a habit, sometimes almost by necessity, to give a first-impulse response rather than a thoughtful response to a question that may have been brewing in someone's mind for a great deal of time. This "automatic" response can feel trite, disrespectful, even bristly to the person listening to you; consequently, you may not be seen as an effective communicator worthy of their trust and best effort.

Make the time to really listen to people—without an immediate response. Reflect on what is being said, or in some cases, not said. If you aren't prepared to answer completely at that time, let the person know you aren't prepared at that time and when you will get back to them. People will respect that honesty in you as a leader. Make sure you do get back with them, though; give them a time or date that you will reconnect with them. Write it in your planner. Don't miss the opportunity for that reconnection. If you miss the opportunity, it is difficult to regain trust with that individual and all those in his or her sphere of influence. The reality is more often than not if you miss that opportunity, you have lost trust with that person forever and with those around him or her.

One of the lessons to be learned here is to not answer or give an opinion too quickly but on the other hand not spend too much time mucking about. There is a fine line between being arrogant and appropriate. A quick response can feel harsh to some ears even though it was meant to inform or soothe, especially if the other person has been agonizing over the issue. Learn to take a breath before responding and actually recite the plea, question, or observation to yourself, in your head, or out loud before responding—it makes a world of difference in the responses you will receive back.

The other big communication lesson to learn is to keep a log or journal to reflect in and on. Notice that I didn't just say "keep a journal" but to reflect on what is written. The practice of journaling is championed by many, including pop icon Oprah Winfrey and others who have discovered that inner strength shines from personal reflection.

You can't improve on something you don't think about. A quick note or thought allows that necessary glance back to learn from both good and improvable moments throughout the day. Keeping a Franklin planner, for example, is excellent. Give yourself five minutes at the end of each day for this personal reflection, before closing the door. Then leave work at work and enjoy the evening with your family. You can't be good to anyone else if you aren't good to yourself; remember your truth of developing your own joy first? Develop the skill of self-reflection as a closing activity to each day.

You are a part of a team, a school community. You are the "head," so to speak; if you feel like you are the tail, then you definitely aren't leading with your best intentions or feeling your joy. As the head, you need to be visible to as many people as possible every day.

Make it a practice to be at the front of the school every day before and after school. Be on the playground at lunchtime or recesses. Make sure you are available at break times for team members to speak with you. Do your paperwork and phoning when teachers and students are in class.

Arrive early and stay late. Be the role model not the voice. You need to provide a 110 percent effort every day, day in and day out. The day you bring 50 percent of yourself to the plate is the day your learning community needed 150 percent of your effort. Don't let a day go by that you didn't do your best. After all, if you don't give your best, how can you expect teachers or students to give theirs?

You have to inspire yourself first, before you can inspire others. Be excited about who you come in contact with and what you will learn every day. An inspired mind is a happy mind, whether it is yours, a team member's, or a child's.

Breed a success-oriented culture on your campus through your attitude, dress, and actions. Life is simple in this respect; do what you expect of others and they will follow your lead. If you don't care about cleanliness on campus, neither will they. If you don't care about what is being taught, neither will they. If you don't dress to impress, neither will they. If you don't take action on your promises, neither will they.

SHARE THE WEALTH

Having so many people within your school, you are rich with resources. Your job is to make sure that everyone benefits from this wealth. Let people know when they are doing a good job—write a note, stop by the classroom, acknowledge the effort being made in a way that is comfortable for you and them. As you do this, though, be aware that someone else might benefit from the skill you have observed.

Encourage people to meet with one another, one to one, before school or after school, or offer to take a class out for PE. People will share individually if they think they are valued and appreciated for their talents. Just telling someone to share at a staff meeting won't work. People generally aren't in a "learning" mode after teaching all day. Learning happens during the school day, for both children and adults.

Share yourself with your staff. Let people know what you enjoy and do it with them; share your joy and passion for education. If you love to read to kids, do it. You may stop by classes just to read a book or chapter from something they were reading or studying. You will receive positive feedback from that practice, and love doing it. Primary teachers can keep a few books on the board ledge for this purpose while intermediate teachers may keep a chapter book in the same place. It is a practice you can really look forward to as a part of your regular day. A colleague of mine loved to play the guitar. He would take classes into the cafeteria each week for a songfest.

Connect with another principal or group of principals. This is the best way to stay grounded in your thinking and understanding of your learning community. Having the ability to share your ideas and thoughts with someone else in the same position is powerful. One very good friend started an assistant principals' meeting once a month when we were "newbies" to share, strategize, and plan. This was an invaluable networking opportunity for all of us at that time. We could share about working with staff, parents, the district office, our families, anything we wanted. We even conducted mock discipline conferences and principalship interviews. Share your professional "self" and people will share back.

PARTNERS IN EDUCATION

Foster enthusiasm for your school with the staff, parents, and the community. You need to fan this enthusiasm into exuberant flames so that creative momentum will grow around your goals of achievement. A book written in 1967, *Enthusiasm Makes a Difference*, by Norman Vincent Peale, holds immense wisdom for us. His words are as true today for education as they were then for sales: "Enthusiasm is no Pollyannaish, sweetness and light, bright and fortuitous concept. It is a strong, rugged mental attitude that is hard to achieve, difficult to maintain but powerful, so powerful!"

Your enthusiasm is optimism for what is now and what is to come. Enthusiasm is an attitude of mind, a mental attitude in a difficult situation. Be realistic and understand clearly that your attitude, more than facts, project the image of the school to staff, parents, and the community. Never let your guard down. Never allow anything to detract from the magic of creativity, believing, and your ingenuity. Ah, but you say, "The test scores are down, the district office doesn't understand." Don't do it. Don't allow yourself to be dragged down that street of pessimism.

Be the positive leader that is tough and rugged, the person who sees every difficulty and faces all facts with your reality. Practice the art of optimism; believe that the good in life outbalances the negative. Your world will always have trouble and problems to solve, look at the opportunities of overcoming trouble and solving problems.

Find a single good idea that will work and work that one good idea. Begin work on it now; don't wait until tomorrow. To be enthusiastic about the idea, *act* enthusiastically about the idea. Using this method of problem solving there is little need to tackle personal or business problems any differently from each other.

Develop a friendship at school. Your friend can be your creative sounding board. At times you may discuss a single idea, then work it through for several hours or even days before it feels "right." These creative planning sessions should be done months in advance of bringing the idea forward to the school community for action.

Development of your year can be based on the four seasons.

- Plan in the fall.
- Work in the winter.
- Create in the spring.
- Implement in the summer.

This year-round school strategy can work for a traditional schedule or year-round with only a weekend separating one year from the next. The only trick to this whole thing is to remember that once the school year starts, it should run as planned, without upheaval and huge changes. Change should be expected and planned for next year.

Minor potholes won't stop the travel to your final destination, but a major collision just might land you, your students, families, and team members, in an emergency room of sorts. Be mindful of what you bring in *after* the year has started; don't create emergency-room situations on your campus.

Grow your team with *your* expectations. Make time to get new team members to observe others on your team. Set them up with your expectations in chunks. Frontload new team members with expectations and models at the end of the school year prior to their starting whenever possible. When new team members join you, follow this sequence:

- Set up visitations and models.
- Set up a series of meetings that include 3–5 items from your "need to know list" each time you meet.

What you personally share should be what you value most in your learning community. Your personal time with each team member as they join your learning community is critical in forming trusting relationships, whether new teachers, clerical workers, aides, or support staff. Take the time up front to do the right thing in establishing your expectations, sharing your culture.

Their need-to-know list might look something like this:

- Your expectations for their success
- Their expectations of you
- Mission statement of the organization
- Deportment—too often forgotten these days—i.e., how you expect them to act (don't laugh, this is critical)
- Information flow
- Where and how to get support
- E-mail / phone etiquette
- Inclusion
- Discipline
- Celebrations
- When and how to notify you
- Setting up their own personal journal
- Asking for ah-ha moments, clarifications, questions, and reflections

Get a drink of water, take a walk, then sit down to think about the ideas presented. Jot your ideas in the boxes provided. By the time you are done, you will have an action plan. This template may be copied and used multiple times for more than one thought.

Chapter 2   Reflection—Plan
Time_____ Date_____

What am I thinking about?	Why am I thinking about it?
What do I want to accomplish?	How can I get there?
Tools/support/people I need:	How will I recognize success?
How will I celebrate?	When will I think about this again?
What do I need to do to ensure my success; whom do I need to connect with?	
How will my mentor(s) know I need support/help?	

Chapter Three

Implement

Implementation begins with *you*. In this chapter you will be looking at yourself, your habits, your beliefs, and your values. Many books have been written; few have brought to bear the truth about implementation. It's all about how *you* view the world. You can't separate your whole being from your position. At the end of the chapter, consider how you will implement the tools shared for the best you.

TIMING IS EVERYTHING (SELF-DISCIPLINE)

As the principal of the school, you need to be self-disciplined. You need to set a model for students, parents, and staff that timing is important. For you to have good timing, arriving at a classroom on time, being at a meeting early to chat, calling that one parent who needs to hear from you today, you need to be self-disciplined. Plan the work, then work the plan.

You need to have the presence of mind to realize who needs what information, and when and how to deliver that information effectively. You need to get all the reports done for the district office and state reports in a timely manner, and you have to tend to your own family.

You need to develop self-discipline. Sketch out the year on a large calendar, highlighting when big reports are due, open house events, any special events. Then back them up two weeks on the calendar as a reminder to make sure everything is ready. Back them up four weeks if you need to check on transportation or meals or special arrangements; send out fliers. Mark an event six weeks early if you need to contact a speaker to review a program or plan an event so it will flow depending on the event.

If you have an administrative assistant, have that person add special classroom events and field trips for you, learning the "backup" method to remind you to ask about the preparations, rehearsals, invitations for the board members and the like. This strategy can be adapted to lengthen or shorten time invested in preplanning. There is no time better spent than in preplanning.

The other part of the self-discipline is making sure you do what you don't necessarily want to do first. Get it out of the way. Take the call you are not looking forward to, write that report you have to write, meet with the staff member who is upset, call the parent who needs to know about a child's behavior; just do it. Don't let these annoyances pile up on your desk or, more importantly, in your mind. You can't focus on the present and maintain your optimism if you are practicing negative behaviors and worrying about the future. Avoidance is a huge red-flag negative behavior. If you are avoiding tasks, either take care of them or delegate them to someone else. Allowing yourself to wallow in avoidance only prevents you from being present to accomplish the tasks at hand.

EVERYTHING IN ITS PLACE (ORGANIZATION)

Speaking of a clean desk, keep it so. Use a file folder system for organization to move things from your desk to the administrative assistant and back again. Folders are marked appropriately for the information they contain; parent concerns, district office, staff, test scores, signatures, media, and the like. Not only are the folders marked by subject but they should be color coded. Color coding information for quick reference and retrieval is key for immediate clarity and organization.

You can teach an administrative assistant to "screen" the mail daily for you then place the appropriate folders on the side of your desk. Pick them up one at a time, review the contents, act upon the contents with a Post-it note, a call, a letter, a date in the calendar or whatever is needed. Then, place it on the other side of your desk for return to the administrative assistant for continued action or filing. Do this every day at the same time, right after student and staff lunches, or a designated "quiet" time.

Do not to keep double files on things. You don't need to keep any files in your office unless they are of a confidential nature for your own personal use. All other information should be kept in files maintained by your assistant or somewhere else, by someone else. Backing up on a "cloud" works beautifully if you have taken the time to set up a file system for your retrieval before dumping things there. Remember, that preplanning idea from before works here too.

In the overall organization of the day with everything in its place, develop a habit of walking the campus early every morning, about 6:45 as an example. It doesn't matter if the custodian was there to clean up after a soccer game or community football or not, walk the campus quietly by yourself each morning. Take a notepad and a pencil with you. If something needs attention, make a note of it to the person who could deal with the situation.

If a door is unlocked, a note to a teacher. If the bathroom has graffiti, a note to the custodian. If a tree root looks dangerous, a note to maintenance and assistant. If you see a new bulletin board up, a note of thanks. If you notice a stack of student papers, stop to peruse and leave a note. Always a note, complete it at that time so it is and ready for delivery to the appropriate person as you walk back into the office area.

Always be at the crosswalk in the mornings before school, greeting students and parents, sometimes staff as they came in late. You don't have to say much about tardiness to anyone when they see you there. They know you are there interested in them having their best day possible. At the conclusion of each school day be back at the crosswalk wishing everyone a good afternoon; reminding students about completing homework, returning permission slips, and foremost celebrating their successes.

By 3:30 plan to be back in your office, skimming an article or two, saying goodbye to the staff, and proofing the staff bulletin for the next day. Write in your journal the last five minutes or so and lock the gates in the front of the school by 4:30 or 5:00. Don't stay late unless there is a special event. No one has *ever* thanked a principal for being at school when no one is there. You don't need to stay late—because the organization of the day, the week, the month, the year, allows you to be free from worry. Every day you leave you know the game plan of the next day; even write it on a common board for all to see as they come in the next day.

PLACE YOUR PRIORITIES WELL (KNOW WHAT YOU WANT STUDENTS TO LEARN)

Being the instructional leader of the school is a daunting responsibility. Take pride in seeing the building blocks of learning in every area of the curriculum, beginning in kindergarten. Believe in a strong academic program. Believe that an academic program brings pride to students and their families. Believe that program can be delivered in a compassionate, humanistic manner that allows for diversity and preference of learning styles while maintaining high standards for all. Believe this is the "art" of teaching. Not every person is cut out to be a teacher, nor can some people be taught the skill. Some people just don't see how a rigorous academic program can meet the social and emotional needs of children; see how they can.

Children learn from strong models. Your job as the principal is to see that the teachers on your staff are the best models and provide the best for your students. Teachers need to model the expectations they maintain for the children. They need to provide samples of work, frameworks for getting there, and constructive feedback for improvement. The whole way of teaching needs to be tailored to the individual child within the group. It is not impossible, it is empowering.

Start by setting clear expectations and providing appropriate frameworks and models that most children will reach or exceed. Those that require more help will have it with the teacher because she has planned the lesson thoroughly.

Planning is the key to a well-run classroom without disruptive, off-task behavior by children or adults. Every minute needs to be planned to allow for the flexibility of students needs. As the principal, your job is to protect that classroom time. Don't allow teachers to be distracted by bells, intercoms, phones, and so on.

You need to set the tone, "I'll take care of the interruptions so your time with students is quality." That is the most important job we do as leaders, protect the instructional time from all distractions, including those you may personally inflict on the campus.

Don't over-schedule drills, assemblies, or intercom announcements; you will be setting a poor example. Start the day with quick announcements after the flag salute. No disruptions unless it is an emergency, period.

Conference with your teachers regularly to discuss the progress of students in specific content areas. Before the meeting let teachers know your expectations. At the meeting share the data even if it is a hunch or perception on your part. During the meeting make a plan of action and follow through. Schedule a follow-up meeting time. After the meeting take any additional notes on what you will do to provide models, resources, support. Always model what you expect from your teachers and students; a positive attitude, a structure for implementation and timely feedback.

PRIORITIZE THE LEARNING (KNOW WHAT THE LEARNING IS, BREAK IT DOWN)

Get to know the standards and expectations by grade level, not because you are to become the expert but rather so you can support your teachers in their goals to educate the children. You need to understand how the curriculum works together to make the pieces fit. Think of each grade level as a piece of a larger puzzle that must fit together, then you can visualize how "tight" the match must be year to year, from class to class. If the pieces aren't from the same puzzle, just imagine—you get the picture, chaos. Unfortunately a child's education can be that chaos if the years don't align.

Conduct your own mini-curriculum audit by grade level. Go into each class within a grade level and just collect a sample of work in the same content area. Analyze the work and match it to the standards. Is it reflective of the standards? Does it "fit" the grade-level standard of practice? Are students practicing at the appropriate level necessary to be proficient in that standard by the end of the year?

Meet with the grade-level team, review your findings, and have an open dialogue. This is not a "gotcha" situation or an exercise of your supreme reign; it is taking a reading, reflecting on current practice to move to the next level together. Make a team plan and work the plan. Follow up with appropriate checkups and recognition of the hard work they are doing; do this, at each grade level, then be ready to start the process all over again. This practice makes for powerful grade-level meetings and meaningful "walk-throughs" during the day. Soon you will discover the next level, grade level to grade level conversations. By that time you can work them into whole staff meetings because everyone is working together, moving as a powerful team.

LET EACH CHILD AND STAFF MEMBER SUCCEED (SUCCESS BREEDS SUCCESS)

There are more ways than we can imagine to teach and learn a concept. We are all teachers and learners at different times on a school campus. We all have strengths and weaknesses, ebbs and flows. It is your job as the leader on campus to bring out the learner and teacher in your entire community. Nurture your teachers; they will nurture the children. Nurture your community and they will nurture you.

Each child needs to be listened to or observed every day so they feel valued and supported. Sometimes it is not their words but their actions or expressions that will hold the key to their best learning. Without success to build on no one can achieve to their potential. Remember this as you coach people to their next best opportunity of growth.

Teachers are your family as well as the children. Listening to them and observing them every day is not an exercise to ride herd over or to beat them down. Noticing and appreciating is a caring expression of support and valuing each team member.

In the Reading Recovery method of reading instruction for the first two weeks of the program the teacher observes and takes notes on each child's learning behaviors and style. If only we were clinical enough in our educational practices to see each child and adult in our environment with that kind of "lens." As a principal you are the cog that moves the machine of learning, teacher-to-child, child-to-child, child-to-parent, parent-to-child, parent-to-parent, teacher-to-teacher, teacher-to-you, you-to. . . . Build on each person's success to build the strength of your community.

Keep mental notes on staff members' and community members' preferences and style. If you can't remember the details, take written notes, use a planner or an electronic device, develop a "coding." Some like to chat before a conversation, some prefer a direct approach, and still others enjoy a story to start your chats.

People have different communication styles. As the principal in a leading/supporting, coaching role you need to know how each member of your team (team member, community, child) learns best. It is a challenge, to say the least, but so worth your while. Keep notes in your planner or journal.

Don't expect people to adapt to your preferred style of communication; not everyone will agree with you—ever. Just know this. Be the conduit to others' success. This makes a great coaching leader. Bring success to every team member by being who and what they need you to be, not the other way around. Often it can be as simple as a sounding board to validate the efforts they are making. But, if you are not physically and mentally "there" for them, those opportunities for success will be few and far between.

Lead by listening first; check your understanding by rephrasing their words and posing leading questions. Often people will come up with their own answers, allowing you to be their ultimate cheerleader and guide-on-the-side. Mark in your calendar the gist of your conversation. In two weeks or so make a note to check with that person and the progress toward their goal. Make time to celebrate their accomplishments. It's about playing their best in your orchestra. A conductor does not play an instrument, she feels and sees each player but ultimately brings harmony by encouraging the players' individual excellence. Be the conductor of your orchestra.

The research of school reform over the years hasn't panned out in the long run. Giving power to the individual teachers, seeking wise counsel from outside agencies, and elevating the principal to the sole instructional leader have resulted in expensive, time-consuming exercises that leave everyone frustrated—politicians, educators, parents, and students. This is similar to the old parable where all species of animals are supposed to learn to fly, run, and swim with the same efficiency as a bird, a cheetah, and a fish.

What works over time is to understand the power of collective teaching; everyone has a part in the whole effort. Developing communication channels with and among teachers results in real trust, creating sustainable student gains. And finally, understanding your role as the "protector," the "parent," and "cheerleader" will catapult your team to developing a high level of job satisfaction and appreciation throughout the organization. When teachers are satisfied and appreciated, they do extraordinary things. Who needs to look for Superman when you work with a team of motivated superheroes every day?

What does being the protector, parent, and cheerleader of the teachers mean? First, to be the front line for your teachers is key. You need to advocate for what they do both on and off your campus. You need to be the connector to the community for them and the person who will take the "hit" first when things don't go as planned. Most of the time you will feel joyful in this role; there are times when meeting with a disgruntled parent doesn't feel good in the moment, but it will ultimately bring joy in developing trust with your team in the long run. These learning times are valuable lessons for you, the parent, and the teacher, for you learn how best to facilitate a solution that keeps the student as the focus.

Being the parent to your staff is truly a blessing and filled with joy when you see your team as siblings of each other. Each sibling has a strength worth developing and usually a weakness that you can either choose to ignore or address. Prefer to address the weaknesses when you see the crack or when it has been shared through the perception of others. If you choose to ignore a weakness, just know that at some point in time it will become an obstacle that the others on the team can't overlook, like the older sister who always gets her way by telling the mom what she wants to hear. The other siblings know better that she is sneaking out at night. Be aware of what the siblings think about and how they treat their own family members.

Don't be afraid to mention what your perceptions are. Unfortunately a group of teachers behaving poorly toward another team member simply because she or he may be different happens. The nucleus group may have lost their group perspective; understanding that team members fulfill differing roles, having a similar but different staff paints a picture of richer diversity for your community of families and for supporting their needs. You need to foster and develop a team of diverse members who don't all see things with the same eyes and ears.

The third way to support the staff is by unabashedly being their biggest cheerleader with the larger community—the families, their peers, and with them directly. A good football game, whether the team is winning or losing, has a sideline of cheerleaders to bring hope, inspiration, and encouragement to make one more score for the team. The cheer squad is not individually calling out numbers to encourage the team in this case; they are inspiring the team to move together. Inspire your team to move together in the spirit of a continual community win. Do this by remaining optimistic, modeling excellence and empathy, and staying fully engaged with them. A cheer squad at a football game is not leading basketball response calls. They are in the game with the players on the field.

Get a drink of water, take a walk, then sit down to think about the ideas presented. Jot your ideas in the boxes provided. By the time you are done you will have an action plan. This template may be copied and used multiple times for more than one thought.

Chapter 3   Reflection—Implementation
Time_____ Date_____

What am I thinking about?	Why am I thinking about it?
What do I want to accomplish?	How can I get there?
Tools/support/people I need:	How will I recognize success?
How will I celebrate?	When will I think about this again?
What do I need to do to ensure my success; whom do I need to connect with?	
How will my mentor(s) know I need support/help?	

Chapter Four

Assess

DO THEY KNOW IT?

Here's a simple question: Do teachers really know what is being assessed and why? If they don't, what chance do you think kids have in knowing what will be measured or expected of them? It takes time to develop an idea of what was actually being assessed at each grade-level. If you take a hard look at what we spend the most time on in class, an outsider would think that filling in blanks, copying, matching, and coloring were high priorities in our system.

How do we measure what society is expecting in order to become competent contributors to society? More intriguing is: How do we foster the development of critical thinking in our classrooms every day? Rarely, if ever, has there been a worksheet constructed that facilitates initiative, creativity, or novelty. These are the "workings" of true learning, the living skills vital for student success.

In this chapter we'll take a look at what assessment is and could be, how to approach it, and how to use it to fullest advantage. At the end of the chapter you'll have time to reflect on your thoughts and use of assessments both formally and informally up and down the structure of your school community.

To take an idea that is out there, to "see it" in a novel way, to approach a problem with a solution no one has ever proposed—these are the keys to true learning. But how to get there in the construct of "school"? We are now presented with the latest standards of proficiency—"Common Core." Do your teachers, children, and parents even have them? The year below and year ahead? Why, oh why not? We are a system of thirteen "grades," K–12.

Children are in a single system to meet an expectation of proficiency, not on individual islands learning floating factoids. If we don't work together, that seamless construct will have hole upon hole, the proverbial dam has no way of holding up against the cracks of indecision, mistaken turns, and lack of continuity.

Fill the holes with the "mortar" of community understanding and support. Share with your community that we do this because next week, next month, next year. . . . Set the stage for ongoing conversations up and down and crossways among the grades and programs. The number of conversations you will have with parents about "content" versus behavior is minimal.

Here's a thought, could it be that the behavioral issues arise because the kids don't know what is expected of them? What are you doing to ensure that teachers, parents, and children know the expectations and how to get there?

Speaking of expectations, are you clear on what they are? Ask yourself these questions regularly. Even keep them in a common plan you will see daily:

- Do I know the mission and vision of my learning community?
- Do I have a personal mission?
- Am I a victim of "mission drift," where over time I have lost the overarching vision and mission of my school and community?
- Do my mission and the vision of the community match? How do I know? Whom have I asked? What outside resources do I track?
- Do the students in my school know what is expected of them? What do I know to ensure they know the expectations?

HOW DO THEY SHOW IT?

A common statement when it comes to performance is "show me what you know." We are all unique; the product will not always be the same. How a student actually gets to a conclusion or solves a problem is of little import to me if the thinking is sound and "works." Student work should not look the same; the eyes that children look through do not "see" the same.

As a country we celebrate the individual while professing that we are united in a common cause. Yes, no, maybe. . . . The lack of appreciation for individuality and creative thought in our schools is real, and because of that there are more and more alternatives to traditional schools. Learning environments, whether virtual or in some sort of brick-and-mortar building, are opening throughout the county and worldwide. People want to learn capitalizing on strengths, interests, and beliefs. No longer are families content with school programs that look like the ones they participated in twenty, thirty, or forty years ago.

My current charter school is a hybrid of in-seat attendance and independent study. Families come from throughout the county and contiguous counties to learn, play, and invent together through personalized experiences that may or may not include classrooms, laboratories, trips, or virtual experiences. They choose when to connect and when to disconnect with the group to develop their life skills of independence, cooperation, competence, and confidence. They are defining who they are in an evolving world that encourages novelty, voice, and possibilities. There is no time in their world to develop skills based on past experience; they are basing their experiences today on the futuristic thinking of tomorrow.

Currently in traditional classrooms we really don't want kids to "look" different or "think" different than their peers. This is nonsense and a far cry from the scenario described based on futuristic thinking. It doesn't mean that we lower our standards of acceptable outcomes either. It simply means everyone knows and can articulate what the expectations are. If a student knows the expectation and it is reached, excellent; if not, you have work to do to ensure their success.

Your teachers are the same as your students. If you don't recognize what is behind the pair of eyes watching you, you can't get them to produce at their best level. If you don't highlight the good and encourage improvable points, nothing will change. If you don't provide the support needed for growth at critical times, it will stop cold in its tracks. If you don't inspect what you expect, it's a waste of everyone's time. Show me what you know, then tell me why.

Tell your audience what you are going to tell them, tell them, then tell them what you told them. This is not a new concept by any means and may even sound ridiculously simple to you, but it is a winning combination every time. Here is what you will do, do it, now tell/show/model for me what you did. Simple, yes? Why don't we do that in our schools? Why don't children understand that expectation from their adult models? Could it be we don't tell them, and worse yet, don't show them the common patterns for making connections and learning? Provide the connections so they can show you what they have done. Be a champion for the cause of your teachers; students will excel and families will be proud.

HOW TO ASSESS IT

Sounds simple, but just tell them. A child, a parent, or staff member, if you are going to assess whether a task is completed or not and to what level, simply tell them. The best way to "tell" anyone is to show them. We have gotten away from using our communication skills of speaking and listening with the advent of electronic communication. In the quick-paced lives we live, we assume far too much when it comes to communication and assessment.

People are left at their desks, in their classrooms or homes, even the districts trying to figure out how to assess their success, often after the fact. Without a way to measure growth firmly in your mind and in the minds of those you lead, you cannot meet your mark, you cannot measure growth, and therefore you never get the opportunity to celebrate success. Those celebrations are key to building accomplishments. In short, if you don't set your team up with expectations, they will feel less than successful.

Rubrics and scales are plentiful and many intelligent people have spent a lifetime of work developing these instruments; rarely are they used effectively. Instead of scales, they are seen as end points. As the leader of your community, select rubrics that have meaning for your team— whether they are developed in-house or not; the key is to use the same measuring piece. Students and their parents cannot follow progress year to year, project to project, day to day, and minute by minute if the expectations are not articulated clearly and consistently.

WHAT IS "IT"?

"It" may be anything from learning how to work in a group, completing a task proficiently, learning how to read, or solving for "x." Just agree as a learning community what "it" is. Keep your "it" consistent. If all students are to read by the end of second grade, say it, measure it, monitor it, and celebrate it. If all students are to be effective communicators, define it and measure it. If anything is worth doing, it's worth celebrating. If you don't want to invest in the celebration of success, then pass "it" up; it's not that important in the scheme of a well-crafted day and plan.

What is the "it" that brings out the passion for learning in your team? Listen to their conversations, in the hallways, in the staff room, and in the community. The "it" is there for you to start with, but it is up to you to identify the task. It may be only one thing or a list of a hundred. It doesn't matter, but whatever you do, focus on one "it" at a time until your team is confident and they feel the success of their efforts. Build upon that success for the next "it." Using the ideas of futuristic learning, looking at dreams and potential rather than studying best practices and models may be the worthiest direction for our time and investment of our resources that bring ultimate joy and engagement to all of us in education.

Assessments are big business and mean big money to publishers, districts, and communities. Know the assessments you use. This may seem crazy, but many principals do not know what assessments are used, how they are administered, and more importantly why they are administered. To improve, we need useful data that will guide us to next steps of improvement. At the same time, data for data's sake is a waste of time.

Know the difference between formative and summative assessments. Know how to determine what assessment should be used effectively in a variety of situations. What is the easiest way to accomplish this task? Ask your best teachers. And, if you don't need an assessment, get rid of it. Don't pile on what is not needed to effect true learning.

As the leader of our community do this for yourself:

- Create a chart of assessments used on your campus by grade level.
- Understand the flow of the assessments.
- Use your calendar/journal to record notes.

- Ask questions and support efforts. Notice where teachers need shoring up for implementation, purpose, use. Fill those gaps, one by one.

Get a drink of water, take a walk, then sit down to think about the ideas presented. Jot your ideas in the boxes provided. By the time you are done you will have an action plan. This template may be copied and used multiple times for more than one developing thought.

Table 4.1.

Grade-level	Name of assessment	Purpose of assessment	When it is administered	How it is administered	How you will use the data to inform instruction
K					
1					
2					
3					
4					
5					
6					
7					
8					
9					

Chapter 4   Reflection—Assess
Time_____ Date_____

What am I thinking about?	Why am I thinking about it?
What do I want to accomplish?	How can I get there?
Tools/support/people I need:	How will I recognize success?
How will I celebrate?	When will I think about this again?
What do I need to do to ensure my success; whom do I need to connect with?	
How will my mentor(s) know I need support/help?	

Chapter Five

Working Smarter, Not Harder

FINDING THE "ART" IN THE "SCIENCE" OF TEACHING

Teaching today may be more of a science (or technology for that matter) than an art, an interesting observation of our profession. When the scales of a balance tip to one side, the contents spill out of the swaying perch. Education has tipped, admittedly, but if you think about it, is it truly the discipline of art or the experimentation of science that has swayed the mighty balances of education? Applying the scientific method day by day, teacher by teacher has all but destroyed the very nature of school, which is to practice and learn the skills necessary for life and society. We have lost the sense of social worthiness, where teachers can effectively learn from one another's work. A teacher will go to a colleague before they run to you for advice; your job is to ensure the art of teaching is exceptional on your campus. You do this by honoring the art of teaching.

In this chapter we will delve into your art. The art of developing the soft skills that bring your community into a place of action and trust. Let's ponder for a moment the discipline of "art."

An artist has the strictest of personal discipline, measuring success by audience reaction to his performance. An artist perfects the most complicated techniques into such simplicity that we, as the audience, see the beauty. Look at a piece of artwork, listen to a song, experience a dance, all so complicated but made to look so easy, so perfect.

Educators need to realize the irony of an artist's perfection. Keep your techniques simple, practice constantly, perfect your craft, and reflect on your performance. An artist does not tire of the mundane rituals of daily practice, perfecting a skill and demonstrating his ability to others. Teachers, administrators, and parents should have the same purpose and conviction of life and purpose in day-to-day rituals with children. An artist maintains focus on his own discipline to accurately measure his progress and achievement.

Do this:

- Simplify your techniques by identifying and using your strongest essential personality traits (listed).
- Constantly practice the essential skills that you can perfect over time.
- Reflect on your performance daily so you can learn and improve on your interactions with all the people in your community.

The real artistry of leadership is developing your "soft skills." Those personality traits that will create an atmosphere of trust with those you work with. This much development of yourself can be intimidating to some and downright crazy to others. I am saying that you owe it to your joy and own development of life skills to understand that a little vulnerability makes a strong, effective leader of the future. If you genuinely like other people, you have a leg up. If you really don't like working with a wide variety of people and accept them at their absolute best *and* worst, then a principalship is *not* for you.

The essential personality traits required for your success:

- Optimism (Always.)
- Common sense (Look for practical, simple solutions.)
- Responsibility (You are the bottom line in your community—*never* throw a student, parent, or teacher under a bus.)
- A sense of humor (Sometimes it's just best to laugh at yourself first or at the situations that arise.)
- Integrity (Recognize that you are "at the top of the ladder" in your learning community; that means, people are interested in you whether you think so or not. When people are interested in you, they may "follow you"; watch your electronic social networking as well as physical networking. Right or wrong, people hold you to a higher standard.)

The essential skills that you can perfect over time and must keep current:

- Empathy (Looks different for various people, age groups, interest groups; there is a great deal to learn from observing and studying traits of differing generations.)
- Teamwork (Always look for and create new ways to connect your team with each other and the outside world.)
- Leadership (Take the time to develop your skills, then mentor those coming behind you; always prepare for their success after you leave.)
- Communication (Stay up on the latest social networking; continually work on your writing and speaking.)
- Good Manners (Really? *Really*. You would be surprised. As mentioned earlier, people are always watching you, even when you don't want them to. The number one acknowledgment you will receive is "thank you for the thank-you note.")
- Negotiation (Your community negotiates very differently group to group. Know how to negotiate in different situations; dare to use a variety of strategies in your daily practice of people engagement.)
- Sociability (Be able to chat it up with parents in the parking lot and lead grand discussions with community leaders and politicians.)
- Teach through guidance and modeling (Be the model and not the voice of learning strategies you want to see in your community.)

OWNING FREEDOM IN A STANDARDS-BASED PROGRAM: DEVELOP A FLOW AND TRUST

To know what is expected and do it well is perfection. Teachers twenty years ago or more had no idea what was expected at the grade level they were to teach. The textbooks didn't tell them, the teacher next door didn't tell, and the principals certainly didn't tell them. They were left on their own—with a pile of grade-level books and an empty classroom. There were no standards for the children to attain, and there were no standards of teaching to measure oneself against. Several people in those years left teaching within a year or two; they were frustrated, disillusioned, and unsupported. Somehow, a few made it through and thrived because of a caring principal.

A teacher may have had a principal who saw potential in him and a friendly teacher with ten years of experience that "showed him the ropes." The principal may have introduced him to his possibilities and crafted opportunities for him to succeed. The principal wouldn't allow him to get too comfortable without giving him that new challenge. She believed in him and told him so. She gave him suggestions to improve; she brought in other teachers to observe a successful technique in "his classroom" as well as encouraged him to see other teachers in their rooms.

She encouraged his ongoing education. Thanks to her, he received his master's in educational administration. Without her he would not have had the opportunities in his career to advance. Without her he would not have obtained an administrative credential. He was motivated not only for himself but because of her, because she believed in him, because she cared. That teacher grew to see in himself what she saw in him—potential. Notice that he didn't recognize his potential first; she did. Just as a parent sees the potential in her child before the child ever realizes it, a strong principal will develop and cultivate the strengths of her team.

Standards for the teaching profession and content standards free us up as educators to measure success consistently. Without them, we simply have an opinion, feeling, or hunch. Big business does not succeed in the long run on opinions, it uses facts that are measured; we need to use data and consistent measurement tools, "standards" to move us forward together.

If a staff member doesn't want to operate with the freedom that a standards-based program brings, you don't want them. Encourage them to move on to be successful in another environment. You are building a team for success with common goals and vision, a safe place for staff members and community to talk about expectations, standards, and improvement.

The debate is dead; standards are here, they are not going away, and they free your creative mind from "the what" to focus on "the how" of education. Living through the days when the debate of "what to teach" took so much energy that it became hurtful, we never got to the "how," and sadly, children did not benefit from the debates; they were robbed of time that could never be recouped in their educational opportunity. Their potential was not developed.

The most intimidating process in education for teachers and administrators alike today seems to be the "evaluation process." It is difficult to get teachers to open up, to reflect on their work, and to openly state that they are working on a particular area whether it be curriculum implementation, differentiation, assessment, discipline, parent involvement, or a myriad of other areas. We can all improve upon something; if not, we might as well be done with life. Working toward a change in the overall teaching culture is difficult but possible if you use your good sense and understanding to shift from the "big E" to the "five e's" of an ongoing process. It doesn't matter if you have a blank sheet of paper or a list of fifty check boxes. Keep your own focus on the following five e's.

1. Empowerment. The process can empower teachers to identify what they want to work on, give you an opportunity to share your vision, and bring you together to work as a team, *If* you set it up that way from the first day of school. Set an expectation, check in on it, measure it, celebrate it together.
2. Empathy. Remember your old evaluations. If you were a product of a standard "Stull Bill" (California language) evaluation process, it was intimidating, really immeasurable. Teachers walked out of evaluation conferences not clear on how they really did and what their evaluator was looking for. Put on your thinking cap and join in the process with your teachers, don't "do it" to them just because it happened to you.
3. Excitement. Be excited about working together. This is one of your most important jobs, creating the best work force you can. Spend ample time before and after the process to plan for and celebrate the victories along the way.
4. Enjoy. Enjoy the process. If you plan appropriately, even in the summer, for your own benchmarks of completion, then the process becomes a part of your year, not an add-on that you need to get done to meet an HR requirement. If you are stressed, your partner educators are stressed; they follow your lead. The "tone" of your body language, lilt in your voice, and choice of words *all* speak volumes. Are you using the opportunity to ease the process?
5. Enthusiasm. Yes, be enthusiastic about the process. Let your team know how excited you are; work to build on their strengths, develop their confidence, and empower them to grow as much, if not more,

than their students. This process begins the first day you meet, every time you get together.

Once you know what a team member's "thing" is, when you see articles, training, or stories, share them openly. Your team will see you as caring about them as persons, not just staff members; they will see you as the team leader. Once you have established this trust together you can do amazing things.

In the freedom of a charter school we don't have to be bogged down by associations or unions that mire the system in unrelenting mediocrity. I like and recommend a self-reflection process of performance review for everyone every year. Of course, just like a parent developing the potential of their child or a coach developing a prize quarterback, you will have more guidance in the initial years of practice for a novice than you will for a seasoned veteran who understands the power of her own reflective practice.

Many large companies use the 360-degree evaluation, which could be helpful in our arena. Now that surveys are so readily available online, it makes sense to have an employee complete a self-assessment followed by one from the principal or supervisor, a peer or colleague, a parent or student. This information can be pooled together into one report easily. What grand conversations we can have looking at this kind of data about performance whether data or perception based. This is the heart of true reflection.

Traditional evaluations do little more than frustrate all associated with them from the employee to the employer. The current processes simply don't do anything to improve instructional practices, and in some cases they water down effort to develop new skills.

For years best practices in education have included triangulation of data when conducting a student study team meeting to determine what should be done to move the learning to the next level for a child. Typically data comes from daily work, unit tests, and summative assessments. This simple triangulation of data makes sense for teacher study as well. I can see a simple triangulation of data agreed upon by the teacher that could look very different, one teacher to the next, as a healthy next step in the development of true self-reflection and teacher improvement.

DEVELOP COACHING, PEER TO PEER

There is a kind of entrepreneurship that is brewing in public education. It can be felt by listening to your teachers, watching marketing of online universities on the television, or by just observing how children and adults learn best. We learn best from each other. Whether your teachers engage person-to-person with campus colleagues or online through any number of social and innovative networks, they are seeking out how to connect with each other. Don't stand in their way! Instead, foster those relationships that will result in increased awareness of content, pedagogy, organization, and student learning.

Find ways to enrich your teachers' cognitive abilities; in turn they will engage students through brain-based insights that will affect learning throughout life. Learning to engage others in meaningful ways will result in retention and application to new challenges. As I have learned over the years, brains are pattern-seeking machines, whether in an adult or child. Create patterns for your team so they can be freed to share with others. I happen to like using numbers and acronyms; they stick with me, and I use them often when sharing stories or practices with team members.

Understand that "school" is changing and when your teachers interact with parents and each other they are creating niches that fit individual kids. This kind of flexibility is forming schools within schools. Agile learning organisms that creatively combine hybrid programs are popping up inside and outside the traditional system. They are developing small learning communities that bring together like-minded learners and colleagues. Whether on Pinterest, Facebook, Twitter, a blog, or university chat rooms, peer-to-peer sharing is thriving and developing a new breed of teachers who understand the need to bring opportunities, not so much content, to their students.

Content is a cheap commodity these days; opportunities to creatively express oneself and receive meaningful feedback are not. Think about regularly posting educational articles, lists, diagrams, and strategies on Facebook or other social media accounts. Why bother? Because those teachers that won't ask you a question will read about what you value and will take action. Between posting things that interest and inspire you personally and family vacation pictures, post information about teaching and learning that you believe in.

Remember your primary job as principal is to facilitate ongoing learning for everyone on your campus. That learning may take place for a team member at midnight when you are not awake, but the cloud delivers your message right on time. Since you are passionate about learning and teaching, it is a fun way to see what resonates with people too. You never know what outside source or sources will come to you to enhance or empower your teachers because of a post or a well-placed comment or question. You are always "on" in that regard, so embrace your ability to share and receive feedback seven days a week, twenty-four hours a day.

Your use of social media is up to you. Even though I don't monitor it every hour of the day, I like knowing that new postings are there when I want them, not to burden me but to offer me valuable information and feedback.

When working with fellow principals it was revealed through sharing that we all manage our e-mails differently; in doing so we either see it as an opportunity for growth or a time-sucking nuisance. Let me just say, manage your e-mail so it doesn't manage you, just like anything else in your day. Skim through e-mails in the morning and in early afternoon after regularly scheduled routines have been fulfilled. Eliminate all e-mails that don't fit the following three criteria, and in this order:

- Information you have requested (helps to fulfill your goals for the day)
- Information or inquiries from colleagues (fulfills their goals)
- Information or inquiries from parents or community members (fulfills their goals)

Create individual file folders set up in your in-box for team members so you can quickly "file" e-mails to attend to when it is convenient for you. You don't have to worry about forgetting them; they just sit there until you are ready to handle them. Schedule time in your planner to deal with requests as needed.

Get a drink of water, take a walk, then sit down to think about the ideas presented. Jot your ideas in the boxes provided. By the time you are done you will have an action plan. This template may be copied and used multiple times for more than one thought.

Chapter 5 Reflection—Working Smarter, Not Harder

Time_____ Date_____

What am I thinking about?	Why am I thinking about it?
What do I want to accomplish?	How can I get there?
Tools/support/people I need:	How will I recognize success?
How will I celebrate?	When will I think about this again?
What do I need to do to ensure my success; whom do I need to connect with?	
How will my mentor(s) know I need support/help?	

Chapter Six

A Challenge to Acknowledge

WHAT IS THE REAL CHALLENGE?

Education is a closed club. Whether it is public or private, education is afraid to show any vulnerability or weakness. As such, we close the doors of opportunity. This is the exact model of what old-guard leaders were taught: don't show any weakness, vulnerability, or personality. Set the course and others will follow. This model has failed miserably in the corporate world of today, yet we somehow don't acknowledge the parallels in education.

We don't listen to our children or their parents. We dictate and hold the system close to our chest. Why? To admit there is a problem is to open the doors to change, to feel the ripples of that pebble in our educational pond. Needless to say, successful leaders realize the necessity for and embrace change, even usher it into their communities. Those who resist change will never truly lead. They may be managers, but they cannot empower others to reach their highest potential. We need bold leaders in education, not managers who maintain the status quo.

Far too many "managers" have reached positions of leadership only to perpetuate what has been instead of innovating for what could be, to dream and bring to life the *big dreams*. This managerial response to leadership is so true in many districts seeing charter schools and privatization as enemies of their systems. Realizing that there may be another way to do school admits a weakness far too few are willing to crusade for or even acknowledge.

WHAT IS YOUR JOY?

Loss of the vision for children and our future, through mind-numbing politics and placating to special interest groups, has plagued our traditional education system for years. Educators have been tossed around in the winds of party politics for so long that our passion for teaching and nurturing the potential of all children has nearly died within the existing system. Educators have a wonderful trait that is a strength and often an even bigger weakness—they are people pleasers. Typically teachers become teachers because they were good students.

Good students figure out the system they experience. If they figure out the system, then it is "their system" to keep, at least that is what most people think in the existing paradigm of education. Well-intended teachers and administrators have formed unions that are destroying public education because they are resolutely clinging to "their system." While good was accomplished once upon a time, collective bargaining is bankrupting the system and avoiding the bigger issue, failing in preparing students to meet their futures with confidence and competence.

Our public education system will crumble under its own weight sooner or later; there is sadly not another option because the system stubbornly won't change. Remember the water cycle shared early on? Without changing the water the ripples remain in the same pond. Without a new vision, a bold plan, a new way to personalize learning for children focused on the future, the system will ultimately fail. Without people volunteering to step out of their comfort zone, uncovering what really doesn't work for kids, we can't move forward.

This is the hard part; we all are to blame and need to take responsibility for the lack of ingenuity and entrepreneurial vision in education. While advocating for victim-like behaviors doesn't help any of us in any situation, taking responsibility for "what is" can move us all forward to ultimately benefit everyone within our living, breathing learning communities called school.

One of the biggest obstacles is and continues to be the "ego" of the system. We all have it; it lives within every organization and human being. As a leader of a team, though, it is incumbent upon you to understand how your personal ego definitely impedes what makes sense for children and your learning community. And if you believe your community is a living organism, it too has an ego that needs to be checked.

You must work every day to leave your ego at the door; stop trying to blame anyone or anything for what is wrong within your learning community; that is not the way to find your joy and excellence. More often than not, if you have a strong negative reaction to someone, something, or a situation, it is because of your own doing. It usually has nothing to do with the person across from you or the situation at hand. Take a deep breath, step back. You are not always a judge to find guilt or innocence but rather the conduit for your team to grow and thrive.

Sometimes you just need to have some grace. It is not a tangible skill but a part of your character worth cultivating when establishing and growing personal relationships in your community. Your joy in leading, teaching, and learning excellence can be something that brings ultimate satisfaction to those in your sphere of influence. When you catch yourself "blaming" anything or anyone, replace your thinking with ownership and see what happens. You feel empowered to make a difference instead of tossed around by the demands of others.

WHERE IS HORACE MANN NOW?

Prior to Horace Mann's travels to Prussia in 1843, the public school system in the United States looked very different from what it looks like today—grade-level manufacturing warehouses. Schools were typically one room. Children learned from other children, older and younger, skills were attained and celebrated according to a child's unique learning style. Once a skill was mastered it was passed on to someone else, whether younger or older. The old idea that you really never know something until you teach it to someone else held true and was honored through mentorships, not through certificates and competency tests. This model sounds a lot like the larger goals of the Internet now, don't you agree?

Learning can take place by anyone at any age, at any time, and any place, developing competencies, showing what you know, and not necessarily receiving advanced degrees. This is the "new" model of learning in today's future-driven society.

In a one-room schoolhouse, models were readily available for a new student, while routines and expectations were established for all learners in attendance. The whole group didn't start and stop at the same point in time, they weren't expected to achieve the same information in the same way or at the same level either.

What would Horace Mann think now? Did he intend to reform all education in the United States to be nothing more than a manufacturing plant that was state of the art in the nineteenth century? Did he ever imagine he would be the end of the road for improving the entire educational system? This model doesn't appear to come close to the personalization required of today's future-focused education. Horace Mann is described as an educational reformer who was not well regarded by the old guard of the day. Isn't it time, after roughly one hundred seventy years, that we reform education to better suit the needs of this generation, not based on what we know from the past?

What is old can be very new again! Children learning from other children, teachers learning from other teachers, parents learning from other parents, make sense? Sure it does. Why don't more of our schools look like this? Why are we holding on to a system that keeps one from another, impeding the synergy of learning as community? I can tell you why: the current "old guard" doesn't like it. But it is the worthiest of efforts for all of us to undertake. Make learning for the future our passion.

When looking at any organism it is the relationship between its cells that drives it. Without relationships and interdependence upon one another we cannot thrive as a system. Think of it yet a different way, though the eyes of a professional sports team. Individual "stars" can be hired for lots of money but if they can't give and take, learn from each other, and work together, they will lose, often *huge* losses. Our educational system is a lot like that dysfunctional sports team—lots of individual "stars" but no "team" to build success.

I think that Horace Mann's educational reform of the 1800s built to tame the "unruly children of the time," ushering them into the manufacturing jobs of their future doesn't exactly produce what is needed now. Bringing all children together in classes to have common learning experiences sounds ideal and should work, but does it really? Perhaps it does: by bringing all children together we have provided the least common multiple to all. Yuck, that is *not* an inspiring *big idea* that people will follow!

Do we aspire to be a least common multiple or an exponent of possibility? Be exponentially excited and inspired from within and without. This kind of thinking inspires brains and brings great joy to the daily work of students, teachers, parents, and leaders.

One of the larger conversations held over the years has been that it's not about maintaining the system, it is providing a comprehensive growing education over thirteen continuous years, not thirteen years of individual experiences. When education is looked at as a system for each child and not a child within a system, opportunities open up for everyone. Doing what is right for children by maintaining your focus on their needs, one child at a time, is tough, but one of the worthiest challenges of your career. Not everyone will like you or agree with you. Doing what is right for kids, moving people forward to find their own success, and building toward the future are reward enough to bring a good night's sleep to the principal focused on excellence.

WHAT CAN WE DO?

Roll up your sleeves and get to work. There are eight steps to taking positive action when a problem of monumental proportion exists, from campus security to disgruntled people to curricular issues to the very system itself:

1. Keep calm. Use your head and keep your wits about you. Know that you don't have to provide an answer right away, unless lives are immediately on the line.
2. Don't be overwhelmed by the magnitude of the problem. Often writing it down on paper so you can look at it diminishes the size and knee-jerk reaction to respond.
3. Break down the issue. Write down every element of the problem you can imagine, all the negatives and, yes, even the positives if they are there. The old "draw a line down the middle of a paper" strategy works wonders.
4. Skip the analysis of the what-if's or why's. This is not the time for victim-like behaviors. Blame games don't work. It is what it is. Own it for the possibilities that exist in the future. John F. Kennedy never would have inspired the landing on the moon if he didn't move beyond what was possible now.

5. Look for a solution, perhaps not to the whole problem all at once but for a next step. Often we want to solve a knotty situation in one fell swoop. Rarely if ever does that work. What is one thing you can do today toward moving forward? But be cautious, without a big enough possibility your mind won't engage and get excited. If your mind isn't excited, no one else will be excited in your plan either.

6. Describe the problem out loud; say it. Listen carefully to your words, often your inner voice will have the answer. State the problem as positively as possible.

7. Ask yourself what is the right thing to do in a given situation, not the "righteous" thing to do. Too often righteousness can be judgmental and inappropriate for the problem at hand. Teaching someone a lesson is not the goal; resolution is.

8. Believe in yourself, keep optimism going, you will work it through.

At the end of the day did you do the best you could using all the information you had? If you did, you will sleep well. If you didn't, you will wrestle with your decision or, worse yet, indecision all night long. If that happens, get up, write down your thoughts. Your writing will be there for you in the morning to consider. We all have peek and valley times. If this is a valley time, notice why it is so and make adjustments to move forward.

As a new assistant principal in a large school within a growing district of nearly forty thousand, a veteran principal and assistant superintendent of curriculum and instruction gave me sound advice. They taught me two very important lessons.

1. The worst thing you can do in this business is to not make a decision. Right or wrong, an honest decision is expected from you. If it turns out to be the wrong one, admit it, correct it, move on. People will respect you for your integrity; no one is perfect.

2. "One monkey don't stop no show." If you think your school can't exist without you, think again. Never think you are irreplaceable. The best leader is a servant to the larger team. Support your learning community, staff, parents, and children, to be their best. Believe that people are good despite the opportunities they will present for you to think otherwise. Be a hopeful optimist, bold in your belief in people.

CULTIVATE YOUR "RICHES"
THROUGH FINANCES AND STAFFING

Two aspects in the business of education you need to be aware of and cultivate are finances and staffing. These twins of different mothers will make you or break you. Understand that in any school—traditionally public, charter, or private—the single most area that will get you in the quickest trouble is finance.

Money is not what you want to mess with, ever. Be above board and beyond reproach in your dealings. Hire someone to keep you on track, to count the money, make the deposits and balance the books. Over time the single most frequent charter school criticism has been the mismanagement of money, because money equals power in the collective mind of society, not the curriculum, the program, or people, but hard dollars and you "sense." Understand that school money is not yours. You are the custodian of public tax dollars. With that in mind be prudent in how you spend those dollars.

Here are some practical differences to keep in mind all the time. Your personal money can be moved around; school money cannot. Your personal money can be invested looking for future returns; school money cannot. Your personal money can be spent on gifts and vacations; school money cannot. Your personal money can be shared as you see fit; not so much with school money. A good rule of thumb has always been this: don't handle money directly. As the person-in-charge, know where the money is going; be vigilant in your expenditures; but more than anything else, ask for what you need.

This entrepreneurial lesson is new to traditional school thinking. Remember, you are a lightning rod for your school community. What you do is magnified in the eyes of those working with you and those who entrust their children and their tax dollars to you.

Do not pinch dollars by auditing your own books. You need a good outside auditor who will review your financial business on a regular basis, more than just once per year. If you don't know how or with whom to start a relationship in this area just ask. Ask those currently working with charter schools; ask local, state, or national associations. There are plenty of people who understand the requirements in this area and will keep you on track. Do not ever think this is an area you can manage on your own.

Money is just too important and volatile; it can be your collapse no matter how good your school is.

Public money is a flashpoint for communities everywhere. If you don't believe me, just look at the number of schools that have been closed or administrators who have lost their jobs because of misappropriation of funds.

Understand the flow of your finances. Find out when your money will arrive, when it will be delayed, and how it is allocated. You can use local, state, and national resources for this critical information. Make sure you develop a working yearly plan for budgeting, auditing, and expenditures. Don't keep it to yourself. Make sure your community understands your attention to detail and responsible behavior. Again, use your planner to keep everything flowing. Work backwards. If the district or county you report to needs a report by a particular date, back up when and who will be working on the information collection and presentation, then intend to have it ready two weeks prior to the deadline. Build in time for research, evaluation, clarification, and preparation of reporting.

Your second "mine" to work is that of staffing. We have discussed the need for a new performance review system, a teacher self-study perhaps, the need for you to develop your team, and strategies to do that. But more to the point is the staffing of your own mind. Think about these ideas:

- Go *big*; little steps don't result in passionate work.
- Trust your gut.
- Don't tolerate small thinking by anyone on your team, especially you.
- Demand more of yourself than you do of your teammates.
- Serve passionately those within your learning community.
- Connect to the people in your sphere of influence.
- Understand you can't change perceptions, but you can change minds with action.
- Activate the best part of yourself because in turn it will activate those around you.
- Learning something new every day.
- Be aware of and personally practice the traits top performers exhibit:
  - Focus in spurts of great energy and concentration.
  - Take breaks and allow others to take breaks.
  - Stay hydrated.
  - Perfect your craft through reflection and realignment.

Staffing in a charter school can and should look different than the local traditional school district. This is one of the areas where the larger community really does want you to take the lead to create a better system.

Parents want the best educators on their team; that is why they have taken the extreme measure of leaving the traditional school systems for the promise of something better. They want excellent teachers who they feel genuinely care about them but, more importantly, care about their children. Their perceptions will make or break you and your community, it really has nothing to do with any systems that you have in place. So, your job as the "skin" of your living, breathing school community, just like the skin of your own body, is to interact with the environment in which you exist.

Learn who the movers and shakers are in your community. Question what statements you hear people make, follow up with your own investigations, and make visible enhancements and changes as needed.

In cultivating your team, share appropriately what the perceptions are and how to celebrate or improve them. Take action on information you are receiving. Understand the relationship between you, your team, and the larger environment (parents and community). Know too when it is in the best interest of a team member to move them to the next great opportunity in their lives. This move may or may not be within your organization.

Your school is not an employment agency; it is a place of learning for the community. If you keep a team member too long, it may jeopardize your standing within the parent community. If you drop a team member too soon, it may jeopardize your standing within your team. It is important to be aware of timing and backlash. There is always some consequence (more negative than positive even when it is needed) when personnel change happens, especially in the middle of the year. The ripples in your organization last for weeks, months, and in some cases, years. Be very clear about a change that you must make; don't take it lightly, don't prolong it, and above all else, take responsibility for the decision.

If you truly have worked with a team member, listened to their concerns, and understood their motivation, and you conclude nothing can be improved quickly enough to serve your community successfully, then coach them up to their next opportunity and move on. Be fair with all who leave. Be sensitive to the immediate repercussions for her family and offer some kind of severance package that takes care of them immediately. This allows you to move forward to provide an improved learning environment and doesn't leave a rejected staff member or misinformed community to go out developing a negative story about your learning community, how they were treated, and why you should not be trusted.

In short, take care of your people, even the people who leave, so they don't become a cancer that needs to be cut out or treated within your learning community at a later time.

Make sure those immediately affected by a change are personally informed by you. Notice the word *personally*, not through an e-mail. Yes, it may feel more expedient and less time consuming for you but in the long run it will cost you more time later if you have to explain yourself and correct misinformation.

Let's take a moment to think about your learning community as a single living unit. Once a person joins your team they become a living cell of that organism that is your living, breathing learning community. Compare your learning community to your own body. Your cells learn unique traits to serve your total living self. One of the biggest challenges for a leader is to understand and develop a living community of unique cells (people) that have specific skills that serve the whole.

Not every teacher will have the same strengths; nor should they, especially in today's schools that require personalization at every level. Not every parent or child will appreciate and respond to a teacher who is direct. On the other hand, not every parent and child will appreciate and respond to a nurturer who desires to talk everything through. It can be a struggle to make sure your staff reflects the needs and desires of your community and not just your learning preferences.

Diversity of personalities brings strength to your learning community, not weakness. Cultivate your strengths to maximize the personalization for your students and their families. You owe it to your community to "see" with your whole being not just your personal ideal. Your goal as a leader of excellence is to inspire your learning community to see and believe in your mission, not to perform all tasks and provide proof of outcomes in the same manner. If you think about all your cells taking on the responsibility of pumping blood to your heart, what would be left to bring oxygen to your lungs? In a living environment all people do not perform the same jobs at the same time, rate, or performance.

Get a drink of water, take a walk, then sit down to think about the ideas presented. Jot your ideas in the boxes provided. By the time you are done you will have an action plan. This template may be copied and used multiple times for more than one thought.

Chapter 6   Reflection—A Challenge to Acknowledge
Time_____ Date_____

What am I thinking about?	Why am I thinking about it?
What do I want to accomplish?	How can I get there?
Tools/support/people I need:	How will I recognize success?
How will I celebrate?	When will I think about this again?
What do I need to do to ensure my success; whom do I need to connect with?	
How will my mentor(s) know I need support/help?	

Chapter Seven

A Structure for Success

A MODEL TO FOLLOW

What is the ultimate "secret"? There is no one-size-fits all. Where did that term ever come from anyway? A T-shirt is either too big or too small, rarely do you find a "just right" fit. The best way to determine the structure of success for you and your learning community is to passionately believe in the future, know what that future is for your community, and know yourself. What will the children in your area be doing in ten or twenty years?

In this chapter you will learn a structure for success on a daily basis that will ultimately bring long-term success. You will learn the ins and outs of following effective models, learning something new every day and planning for the future.

How will you know that you have accomplished success? Have you asked the community leaders, the businesses, and parents? If you have an outcome in mind, you can plan backward by design. Seriously, it sounds so simple, but it's not; people "skip" this all the time in favor of "jumping in" to fix a problem that may or may not be a problem at all.

Our schools' mission is to partner with parents to develop thinkers, communicators, and achievers.

My vision for our elementary schools is that students will be prepared citizens for high school, any high school. To me, that means they must read, calculate, write, and think in a way that can be applied to any content area in a competent manner.

What is a competent manner? Understanding our children are in a system of thirteen years that should be progressive and not individually planned, what are ninth-grade teachers expecting? Where are the models of competence they expect to see? What are the indicators of a competent and confident learner? Go to those that are ahead of them, study them, then work backward.

A strong practice to follow is to identify those you admire. For instance, there are two school districts in the state of California that seem to have the pulse for where the state is headed before the rest of us get there. One is in the south and one in the north. It's a good practice to follow and to model what you respect.

Get out of your chair and do an observation, make a phone call, take a colleague to lunch. "The" model for you is not the model for your neighboring school, because you have different strengths, different team members, different students, and different challenges. What *is* the same is the goal to achieve excellence, not the map to get there. Keep your eye on that goal; demand it in your own life and others will follow.

Know what excellence for your community looks like and be able to articulate it. Here's an example. In kindergarten students will be able to follow text left to right and identify ten sight words. In first grade students will read three to five sentences of simple text and identify one hundred sight words, and so on. So, you can then have conversations with teachers, parents, and students about something concrete, not about "style" but about "content."

There is true freedom in the use of standards to foster and celebrate artistic teaching! Center your conversations on achievement of the intended goals. Never change a goal without the community being on board. People don't like change, but change happens faster than we realize, often without recognizing subtle shifts. Anticipate it; plan for change and help people to see change and how they are a part of it. Plant seeds to grow in the next season, keeping your thinking ahead of where your community is so change is a natural evolution, not abandonment of the known.

As the principal, you are the change agent of the school. Your team can be ready for change, seeing it as opportunity, or they can see it as an enemy to avoid, ignore, and bash. Your attitude is the cornerstone of implementation. Simply put, without you on board, a new idea cannot move forward. Dreams brought forward have life or death based on your beliefs, words, and actions/orchestration. You possess enough power to make something wonderful happen and enough influence to stop an idea cold in its tracks. Wield your power for good.

The transition from traditional schools to charter schools ten years ago opened my eyes to the possibilities of choice, to choose the "Food Pyramid" of my choice. No longer were the district procedures the expected rules; now was the "roll-up-my sleeves" and *create* time, not only the rules but the actual game.

The entrepreneurial element (futurism) of education has been lost in the traditional educational system. The single most valuable aspect of charter school education is entrepreneurship, the creation of options. Flattening out the "pyramid" of hierarchy by creating a basketful of possibilities for each learner has brought boundless joy to our learning community. One favorite question to ask a parent or teacher mired in his or her own thinking about an aspect of learning is simply "why"? You would be surprised how many people do something based on a perception or set of perceptions, not facts.

An educator with a heart for kids and a mind of sound business practices is a valuable resource in a charter school. The model is simple, if the heart for children is genuine and the lack of ego is real, you can learn to be an effective communicator leading with your passion and joy. To be an effective principal you must understand and believe in the idea of servant leadership. You are the servant of the people you have the privilege to work with. You touch hands, look into eyes, listen to words, feel the air, and taste the lives of those around you. Tangible, real, human stuff is what leading a school is all about.

Keep the big picture in mind:

1. Be passionate about what you do; you will bring joy to others.
2. Understand and value the unique aspects of all individuals you work with.
3. Play to your strengths (not literally "yours" but your community's).
4. Be genuine and optimistic (being realistic doesn't have to be a downer).
5. Live in integrity (not everything you do will be perfect, but intention is *huge*).
6. See each day and challenge as an opportunity, not a problem.

7. Stay focused, plant seeds, till, harvest, and replant; your growing "season" is 365 days a year!
8. Be kind to others, and most of all to yourself

Everyday establish your common ground and pivot points:

1. Do what you least like *first* ("eat a frog for breakfast").
2. Be visible.
3. Be personable.
4. Be attentive and watchful.
5. Be celebratory (write notes, give "high-fives," make phone calls, smile, share stories).
6. Be a planner backward by design; always have the end in mind, even if it is only the day.
7. Be reasonable. Follow-up, take notes, and set dates for yourself; check back, schedule time to process things, but don't forget what you have "on the burner." A pot of rice *will burn* if you aren't mindful of the time.
8. Be a connector. Make connections with your community; assume your position as a public official boldly and respectfully. Don't take your position for granted.
9. Be efficient. Touch paper, e-mails, voice messages, texts only "once" if possible. Everything should have a place to go for an action to be taken, even if it is "to the trash."
10. Be objective. Suspend judgment when you can. You only hear one side of a story at a time.
11. Be tidy. Keep your desk clean. I kid you not; this is a "biggie" for how "approachable" you are. If your desk is full of "stuff," team members often see you as "too busy" to talk with—a missed opportunity for sure.
12. Be ready. Plan for tomorrow before you leave today; count each day.
13. Be "with it." You expect others to have "it"; now you do "it." "Eyes in the back of your head and ears on your feet."
14. Be calm and consistent. Team members and community want to and need to depend on your "charting the course," keep your true north!
15. Be who you are. Don't try to be the leader you think you should be, develop the best *you* can be with your strengths and gifts.

Use your planning time wisely. Planning time for you is when school is not in session and teachers are away. This means that winter and spring breaks as well as summer time are your peak times to plan. Understand that, and work your year around those prime times for planning. Abraham Lincoln has a quote that goes something like this "If I had just six hours to chop down a tree, I'd spend four of those hours sharpening my axe." Now that's a planner! Every minute you spend in the planning phase helps the actual event run more smoothly. Here are tips that have been perfected over the years.

Summer Time

First, do it by the numbers. How many days in your school year, semesters, quarters, units? In this case we have 180 days of school: two ninety-day semesters, four forty-five-day quarters for the high school, and six thirty-day units of study for the K–8 program. Every day is numbered on the calendar in the summer, so we know exactly how many days we have been in session and how many days we have left. There is something to be accomplished every day we are in session. Label your days so you are clear the clock is ticking.

Second is to schedule everything you can think of, writing it on your calendar, including:

- Audit/business deadlines
- Any required district deadlines
- Staff meetings (approximately once per month); create a template to use throughout the year
- Staff celebrations (potlucks and major holiday luncheons)
- Student assemblies
- Student recognition programs
- Ordering of resources, materials, supplies
- Writing evaluations
- Team member birthdays and special event anniversaries
- After-school programs
- Community meetings
- Writing of your monthly accomplishments (end of each month); create a template to use throughout the year

- Updating your end-of-year report (four times per year), with a template to add to throughout the year
- Updating your web-based resources (I schedule every Monday)
- Writing your weekly parent e-mail (written on Wednesday, posted each Friday), with a template you can just drop information in each week
- Writing weekly message to teachers/community (written on Thursday, posted each Friday); create your template now, then number and keep in your files on your computer
- Organizational meetings (i.e., calendar committee, grade-level committees, staff development opportunities)
- Testing windows
- Club meetings
- Student performances
- People to regularly "reach out" to—your mentors or mentees, movers and shakers within your learning community
- Even schedule "think time," where you can read anything you want or not (once a month)

Next make sure you have backed up your lead-in time required—two weeks, three weeks, a month, six months—add to your daily tasks to build up to an event.

Then set up required files on your desktop, create templates for meetings, mailings, and so on. Anything that can be done ahead of time needs to be touched and planned for at this time. This is the time when people are not your priority.

When teachers and families come back in August, they are on-board. You have the "frame" set so they know now to schedule/plan their days. Nothing will get you more off base quicker than to throw something at your team members or community after the year is rolling. Unless it has dire impact, don't change something mid-stream.

You now have the time to spend with your people and community when they need you and expect to see you. You aren't creating or managing anything "new"; the blueprint is ready to go. You are ready to engage with the people in your learning community—teachers, parents, and students—*now*. People become your priority.

Winter Break

Think through where you have been and where you are going. Everything should be on automatic pilot for you at this time of year.

Now is the time to take stock of what is working, what you want to change for the next school year and what resources you will need.

This is the "list-making" phase. Make lists of anticipated staffing, resources, programs, and budgeting priorities. In addition to lists, write letters that will be needed. Create a template for letters too: a parent letter for spring standardized testing, a thank-you letter for donations, a letter of congratulations for students.

Spring Break:

Check your winter lists. Is everything on the table and communicated for staffing, budgets, and resources? Is everything ready for the end of the year? Create end-of-year lists as needed. Once school is back in session it is a mad dash until June to get through mandated testing, to celebrate accomplishments, and keep one foot in the current school year while one foot is firmly planted in the future.

Five resources you must have at your fingertips for your success:

- A calendar of your choice that parallels your school year (July–June): a Franklin Planner or any system that works for you.
- A personal journal (can be a part of your calendar, which is my preference).
- Individual teacher conference form (see sample below). This will keep your conversations focused and includes follow-up. Make multiple copies to have handy.
- Your Pivot Success Traits (list). It is important to keep an eye on your performance. Send a monthly update to a director each month or someone whom you feel accountable to.
- A Typical Day (see sample below and a template for you to develop your own)

PIVOT PLANNING FOR EXCELLENCE

(A template to use when setting up a new program, solve a problem, work with your team)

Time_____ Date_____

What am I thinking about?	Why am I thinking about it?
What do I want to accomplish?	How can I get there?
Tools/support/people I need:	How will I recognize success?
How will I celebrate?	When will I think about this again?
What do I need to do to ensure my success, whom do I need to connect with?	
How will my mentor(s) know I need support/help?	

Individual Conference Form

(write as you go, fill-in afterward. Just remember to keep it simple, direct, and have an actionable result that can be measured)

Name_____ Time_____ Date_____

What we are examining	Why we are examining it
What we want to accomplish	How we can get there
Tools/support needed:	How will we recognize success?
How will we celebrate?	When will we meet again?
What do I need to do to ensure your success/support your efforts?	
How will I know you need support/help?	

Your Pivot Traits of Excellence

Just as students and teachers need to know what the expectations of an assignment are, you too need to know the expectations of your "assignment." Refer to this list. Put items on cards or at the top of each month. Assess yourself regularly.

1. I passionately hold a belief in my schools' mission; it is highly visible/felt throughout my school site across all community members. It's a feeling I promote, not words I post.
2. I focus on school practices and goals aligned to the school identified mission and vision. It's a tone I promote and celebrate.
3. I insure time is spent on important things: student achievement, common expectations, collegial work, and celebrations. I don't just schedule meetings.
4. I know essential standards have been identified by the school community and are measured and used routinely by me and my team when discussing student achievement. I have a clear understanding.
5. I monitor the teaching of grade-level standards including use of the adopted resources and instructional materials; use of common assessment instruments and feedback techniques are ongoing. I make personal connections as well as my team.
6. I insure that instructional time is not interrupted except in extreme emergencies. I don't allow fire drills or assemblies or request answers of my team members to my questions during instructional time.
7. I appropriate sufficient resources to instructional programs. I keep the money closest to the kids.
8. I develop and maintain appropriate interventions for my learners. I connect options and choices based on student needs.
9. I develop a supportive system to provide appropriate feedback to teachers, staff, and community. I am available when they need me to be available.
10. I build a community consensus about the importance of specific learning for all students. I tend to my "garden," throughout all seasons.
11. I use a variety of techniques to extend continual learning to all team members.

12. I embrace technology to allow for ongoing learning. I am a model of continuous learning.
13. I participate in collegial work with other leaders. I am honing and advancing my vision for success, to be a part of something bigger. I have selected my own mentor, whether formally or informally, to whom I hold myself accountable. I seek regular feedback.
14. I invest my personal time in conversations with teachers and parents about student achievement. I create time for others.
15. I believe I make a difference in the lives of those I work with every minute, every hour, everyday. I believe in the future and invest in it daily using forward thinking.

To keep yourself on track, send an accomplishment e-mail to someone you hold yourself accountable to each month. Not because it is asked for, but because it holds you personally responsible for the vision and implementation of the big ideas at your school. The task reframes your thinking about what your long-term goals are and what progress you are making toward them by establishing and meeting regular goals. It also gives you an opportunity to report on what you know your superior values and desires to report to the board of trustees on a monthly basis. You should know when this report goes to the board members so you submit your report at least a week before. It pays to know the flow of information up and down your organizational structure.

A TYPICAL DAY: DAILY FRAME

For this frame notice the bold and regular print. The bold words frame the day, basically staying the same one day to the next. The regular font represents the shifting sands of a typical day that may change depending on your needs and the needs of your community.

Think of your day as a box. Think of it with defined edges and open, fluid space between those edges. As the leader, plan to define your edges with a routine, then move within the box as needed throughout your day. The time you have as your own is before staff members arrive and after they go home.

Teacher time is before the kids arrive, recess, lunch, and immediately after school. Student/parent time is the heart of the day. Working with families and students at the point they need you is key to your success. A principal's days are long, you need to be there before anyone else and you need to leave after everyone else, or most everyone, to have the greatest impact. Remember you are not a manager of time but a leader of ideas.

Once your habits are established, of course, from time to time days will warrant deviations, but generally a day is nine to ten hours; maintain the practice of being the first and last on your campus (or nearly so). Number each day as a reminder that every day has the potential to be the *best*, most productive day yet.

5:00 Wake up; daily home routine.

6:15 Check voicemail and text messages for anything needing imme-diate attention (e-mails wait).

6:45 Leave for school.

7:00 Arrive at school and begin to *smile*. Survey parking area. Open front door, walk around building, take notes, turn on heaters, lights, check the classrooms for new displays or student work to compliment—write notes and deliver/post as you walk.

7:10 Sit at desk, open computer, review day on white board and in calendar, make any notes, quickly review and assign e-mail to later time, file, or trash.

7:30–8:00 Do the one thing I am least fond of—a report, a phone call, a letter, an agenda.

8:00–8:30 Read articles, welcome staff members as they arrive, look them in the eye.

8:30–8:45 Walk around the school, make sure everyone is in their place, smile, encourage, assist, etc. Touch, Look, Listen, Feel, and Taste.

8:45–9:00 Be outside as kids and families arrive, *smile*, greet, meet, be happy.

9:00–9:10 Quick walk around campus, all students in place, get the "pulse" of how teachers are doing. Check back with those you have a "feeling" about at their break.

9:10–10:00 Answer phone calls, return e-mails, texts, check calendar, plan, check up.

10:00 Check in with your support staff at least once per week. We hold a twenty-minute meeting once a week. but chat daily with everyone.

11:00 Walk out to the playground, just Touch, Look, Listen, Feel, and Taste; use all your senses.

11:15 Walk through classrooms, take notes, celebrate something, talk with kids Touch, Look, Listen, Feel, and Taste; make connections.

11:30 Stop by staff room, chat with teachers on break.

11:45 Answer phone calls, e-mails, etc. Talk with parents, community.

12:45 Have lunch. Visit with staff.

1:30 Walk around campus, chat with kids, Touch, Look, Listen, Feel, and Taste.

2:30 Reflect on your day, so far. Take some notes, thoughts, reflections.

3:00 Be available to chat with parents.

3:15 Be out front for dismissal—Touch, Look, Listen, Feel, and Taste.

3:30 Come inside, jot notes as needed.

3:35 Meet with teachers as needed.

4:00 Plan for next day and week: all materials necessary are ready, reminders on white board, positive intention set. (I use a rotating calendar with leadership quotes on my desk; use whatever works to keep you inspired.)

4:30 Leave (smiling because you were a pivot today, you made a difference).

Develop your own "Daily Frame" Template

- What do you expect to "accomplish" everyday consistently?
- What will you do, and when, each day, from start to end? Remember to keep the end in mind, whether it is a big project or establishing the routine of your day. Be purposeful in all that you do. If something can be delegated, do so and recognize your team members' accomplishment. Keep your eye on each day as the opener and closer of a good series. Everything is done on purpose.
- Build in time to connect with people every day. Staff, parents, community members, students.
- Schedule time to "eat your frogs," the things you least like doing. You'll always find time to do those things you enjoy!
- Keep track of your days—they will race by in a blur if you don't notice and honor them for the potential they have. Nothing extraordinary was built on a "special day," everything starts with an idea; time is added to

let it grow. Number every day of the year, forward and backward. If you have 180 days of instruction in your year, then the first day is 1/179. If you have a week of training before the actual school days begin then the first day is -5/180.

Get a drink of water, take a walk, then sit down to think about the ideas presented. Jot your ideas in the boxes provided. By the time you are done you will have an action plan. This template may be copied and used multiple times for more than one thought.

Chapter 7   Reflection—A Structure for Success
Time_____ Date_____

What am I thinking about?	Why am I thinking about it?
What do I want to accomplish?	How can I get there?
Tools/support/people I need:	How will I recognize success?
How will I celebrate?	When will I think about this again?
What do I need to do to ensure my success; whom do I need to connect with?	
How will my mentor(s) know I need support/help?	

Chapter Eight

Just Do It with a Big Picture in Mind

Times of growth are beset with difficulties. But these difficulties arise from the profusion of all that is struggling to attain form. Everything is in motion: Therefore, if one perseveres, there is a prospect of great success.

—I Ching

IS REAL CHANGE POSSIBLE?

Increasingly, the issues that affect business and education are global in scope. Organizations are nested in a storm-tossed sea of global change where everything affects everything else. Issues of cross-cultural commerce, global economic shifts, resource constraints, ecological impact, and geopolitical (in)stability are redefining the context of leadership. Our old ways of thinking and leading are not capable of encompassing the level of interdependence and complexity we face. They simply are not up to the challenges of global change. In fact, we are barely up to the challenges of organizational change.

A study of more than a hundred companies engaged in major change efforts demonstrated that 85 percent don't yield tangible much less durable results.

Why such dismal results?

Meg Wheatley, renowned author of Leadership and a New Science and a Leadership Circle faculty member, suggests that: "Most of the ways we were taught to think, to reason, to understand simply don't give us the means to make wise decisions anymore. We don't know how to be wise stewards of the dilemmas and challenges that confront us daily. We were not taught how to make sense of a chaotic world, or a world-wide inter-connected web of activity and relationships."

CAN WE DO BETTER THAN A 15% SUCCESS RATE?

Yes, but only if we manage change in an integral way addressing all inner and outer demands. Success is possible, if we are willing to:

- Personally go through the same transformations (fundamental shifts of mind and heart) that we want and our communities are demanding for our schools.
- Engage in the difficult ongoing dialogue that brings to the surface that which is hidden in our culture and allows personal transformation to translate into cultural and systemic change.

We live in a time of great opportunity and potentially great peril. The next fifty years are going to be challenging and beyond the understanding of today.

We could well bring into being a global order going beyond national-ism to serve planetary welfare. We could even destroy ourselves. Clearly the business of education, with its growing global reach, plays a major role in the world's future. It has a huge presence in the potential outcomes of society.

The challenge for leadership in this millennium is huge. Einstein made the challenge for us as clear now as it was when he said it: "The signifi-cant problems we face cannot be solved at the same level of thinking we were at when we created them." Something in our consciousness must shift in order for us to be able to see how to act in a way that can address the challenge of the times.

Be bold in your joy for what you do every day and others will follow in your excellence. Never underestimate the power of a single thought to imagine a new tomorrow. We are the visionaries of our children's future today. If not us, then who?

I had three assumptions about you at the beginning of this book:

1. You were invested in the future of education.
2. You wanted to personalize learning at every level of education.
3. You were willing to work with the one person who can make the most positive gains in your school and your career, *you*.

We explored and developed the immeasurable but palpable "soft skills" to propel you to new heights of fulfillment and joy. We explored the development of your own good habits of thinking. You learned how to work a plan for success. You were introduced to a structure for daily success to keep you balanced and flexible on the "sand" you will walk in everyday to remain pivotal with team members across your community from students to teachers, parents and peers.

No other time in education has been more important for leaders to develop their own skills to lead people into an unpredictable future. It is the most exciting, explosive time in our history; to focus on what cannot be seen but rather felt in the tidal waves of change.

In closing, here are five pivotal questions to check in with personally and with your team on a regular basis, every day.

1. What is my mission today to move my "teaching/coaching" to a higher level?
2. Am I demonstrating bold enthusiasm when I engage others, adults and children?
3. Am I living my own truth? Do I understand the synergy of community? Do I have an image of a parent standing beside each child when I interact with them? Do I see a partner standing tall next to every individual I speak with?
4. Am I taking care of my body? Am I rested; fully hydrated; and sleeping, eating, and exercising enough to have the energy I deserve to have a positive influence on others?
5. Am I demonstrating passion and compassion for right now?

BE the **PIVOT** Principal
Maintain **P**ersonal
Integrity in all actions
Share your **V**ision
Develop **O**ptimism in your daily interactions
Be **T**houghtful of others and yourself

Chapter 8   Reflection—Just Do It
Time_____ Date_____

What am I thinking about?	Why am I thinking about it?
What do I want to accomplish?	How can I get there?
Tools/support/people I need:	How will I recognize success?
How will I celebrate?	When will I think about this again?
What do I need to do to ensure my success; whom do I need to connect with?	
How will my mentor(s) know I need support/help?